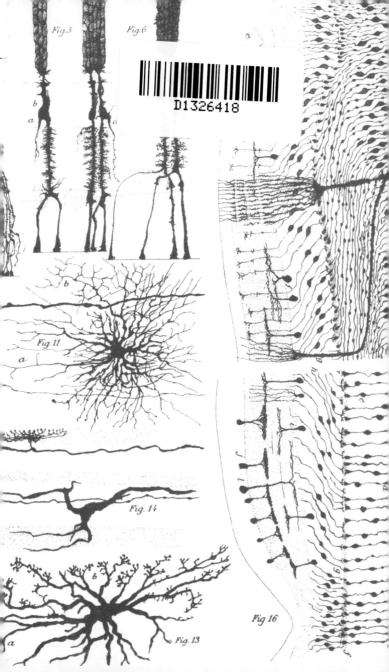

Fig.5 Fig.6

Fig.11

Fig.14

Fig.13

Fig 16

10
VOYAGES
THROUGH THE
HUMAN MIND

Also in the Christmas Lectures series

10
VOYAGES
THROUGH THE
HUMAN MIND

CHRISTMAS LECTURES FROM
THE ROYAL INSTITUTION

CATHERINE DE LANGE

FOREWORD BY ROBIN INCE

Michael O'Mara Books Limited

First published in Great Britain in 2019
by Michael O'Mara Books Limited
9 Lion Yard
Tremadoc Road
London SW4 7NQ

Papers used by Michael O'Mara Books Limited are natural, recyclable
products made from wood grown in sustainable forests. The
manufacturing processes conform to the environmental regulations of
the country of origin.

ISBN: 978-1-78929-097-4 in hardback print format
ISBN: 978-1-78929-129-4 in ebook format

1 2 3 4 5 6 7 8 9 10

www.mombooks.com
Follow us on Twitter @OMaraBooks

Typeset by Ed Pickford

Cover design: Anna Morrison

Endpapers: drawings by neuroscientist Santiago Ramón y Cajal
from *The Retina of the Vertebrates*, published in 1894

Printed and bound by CPI Group (UK) Ltd, Croydon, CR0 4YY

CONTENTS

FOREWORD

by Robin Ince

I was eating an egg and cress sandwich in the company of two acrobats, a neuroscientist and a raven. The acrobats and neuroscientist were new to me, but I had met the raven before. His name was Brann and he once outstared Professor Brian Cox while showing off the shimmer of his black feathers, as if goading Brian's tamer locks. I was backstage at the Royal Institution and about to take part in one of its Christmas Lectures. I was there to be silenced for the purposes of science.

I was the perfect subject for a demonstration for the 2017 Christmas Lectures by Professor Sophie Scott. It can be hard to shut me up. I am overly verbose and nervously chatty, especially when in front of an audience. I seldom volunteer for silence.

Sophie had telephoned me a few months before to ask if I was willing to have a magnetic pulse to the left-hand side of my brain, which would briefly disable the motor region in charge of my vocalizing. She felt that if she could stop me talking then it would prove you could stop *anyone* talking. I volunteered immediately without the slightest glance at the health and safety form. I trust neuroscientists which, looking at some of the more lurid and haphazard experiments of the twentieth century, may not be entirely advisable.

A few weeks later, after taking part in some trial magnetic pulses in the lab, I sat in front of 400 young people in the Royal Institution's Lecture Theatre and recited Lewis Carroll's 'Jabberwocky'. Somewhere between 'gyre and gimble' and 'mome raths outgrabe' I felt a sensation like a low voltage spark hitting my scalp, and the words I was about to say seemed to get stuck in my throat. It felt as though my brain glitched briefly, before starting up again. During each trial run, I found the words got stuck in different ways – sometimes I could feel them waiting to exit, other times they vanished in a haze, but each time only for a moment. Each slight change in positioning of the pulse changed the experience of losing the ability to speak.

Afterwards, some people suggested I should have felt worry or fear in those moments, but my fascination with the brain and the jiggery-pokery that can mess with it usurped my anxiety. It was a fascinating insight into the fragility of the brain and a window, though obviously only a very small one, into imagining the experience of those I have known who have suffered a stroke.

I have been fortunate to take part in a variety of psychological and neuroscientific experiments by dint of being the co-host of The Infinite Monkey Cage series on BBC Radio 4. If anyone approaches me on a late-night train and asks if I would be interested in partaking in a scientific experiment, I more often than not say yes. This is how I found myself at the Royal Hospital for Neuro-disability, having an EEG (electroencephalogram) that gave me some sense of how my brain reacted to the music of the Lighthouse Family. It is why I agreed to an fMRI (functional magnetic resonance imaging) and had my brain scanned as I played a solo game of *Just a Minute*, so researchers could see if anything of interest goes on inside a performer's brain when they are improvising nonsense. It is a remarkable thing to observe the brain where the *youness* of you resides.

We are told that the human brain is the most complex thing in the known universe, so it is no surprise that some of the answers to why we are as we are – a self-conscious creature, able to contemplate our reflection and experience the anxiety that goes with awareness, as well as the joys – are not yet forthcoming. The twentieth century is mired with ambitious experiments that were meant to solve individual cognitive issues, but which often made the patient worse ... or dead. As the knowledge of the hardware inside our brains has progressed, our understanding of why we are the way we are is gaining colour and context. There is much hot debate between neuroscientists and in the heat, some of the flames illuminate us while turning other ideas to ash. If we are to survive as a species, we must find ways to understand ourselves better, to comprehend our decision-making, our will, to know why our brains and minds behave as they do.

I am fascinated by the universe; why atoms behave as they do, what happens at the event horizon of black holes, whether there are many universes. But most of all, I am fascinated by our insatiable curiosity as a species and why we have a brain that has a potential that goes so far beyond survival simply for survival's sake. And that is why I'm glad you have picked up this book, which illuminates through these Lectures how our understanding of ourselves has developed, and gently interrogates our brains and our minds.

I'll shut up now before the magnetic pulse is needed to stop my words.

INTRODUCTION

If a Christmas shopper were to stray off the busy streets of London's Mayfair on a December day, they might well stumble upon a very different kind of festive preparation. With the grand pillars of the Royal Institution building at 21 Albemarle Street partially obscured by huge green broadcasting trucks, they would likely find a camera crew dragging their kit and cables among a flurry of activity, all sorts of props and machinery being delivered, and perhaps a queue of young people waiting to get in. Time it right, they might even spot an exotic animal or two.

Similar final preparations for the Royal Institution Christmas Lectures have been happening here for almost two hundred years (except for a short break during the Second World War). They were dreamed up by Michael Faraday in 1825 at a time when there was scant provision for scientific education at school, and to this day an eminent scientist steps out each year with the mission to enthuse and thrill a bright young audience (many a Lecturer was themselves drawn into science after sitting among the audience as a child). Each series of Lectures is traditionally packed with demonstrations, explosions and unlikely guests and has, since 1966, been regularly broadcast on television. They are also now available for all to watch online, and when the London show is wrapped up, they travel to many locations around the world, reaching hundreds of thousands of people.

Despite this long history, the subject of the human mind only appeared on the line-up rather recently. Brain sciences are relatively young, especially in comparison to physics and chemistry, which were the subjects of the Lectures for much of their early years, and the first Lecturer to tackle the brain head on was Baroness Susan Greenfield – the first ever woman to give the Lectures – in 1994 (see Chapter 7). But the mind is a slippery concept, encompassing much more than the mechanics of the brain itself, and extending also to our perception of the world around us, our thoughts and feelings, intelligence, personality and ultimately our sense of self.

In various forms, these diverse subjects have indeed featured in the Christmas Lectures as far back as 1926 where this book begins. As a result, many of the journeys we take within these pages might seem to start far from the brain and arrive there only towards the end. Others begin inside the head but take us further afield, for instance asking whether our own minds might ever merge with machines. Some delve into our evolutionary past or turn to our interactions as a society to shed light on the special ingredients that make our human minds unique.

This is the third book in the series. The first, *13 Journeys Through Space and Time*, took us from our home on Earth on an adventure into the universe. In the second, *11 Explorations into Life on Earth*, we stayed closer to home, discovering the no less exotic diversity that inhabits our own planet. Here, we journey to a place that should be more familiar still, the corridors of our own minds, and yet the more we try to understand about this subject, the more our world appears upside down (sometimes quite literally).

Each chapter is based on a series of Lectures that would have taken place over several days. For many there wasn't much by way of historical records, and so the material has been drawn from books, notes and pictures. Rather than a comprehensive report, the idea is to revisit some of the most interesting themes and accounts of the science at the time that ultimately shaped our understanding of the mind.

This book tackles some huge questions. What does it mean to be human? How does the brain give us a sense of being? Can we ever trust our own experiences? We also gain an understanding of how the brain actually works, what happens when things go wrong and how that knowledge can be used to help those with neurological problems.

Guided by the best and brightest scientists of the time, the young audience will often become the subject of the demonstrations themselves and so this journey should leave them – and us – with a renewed sense of wonder about the incredibly complex and adaptable organ in our heads that makes us who we are.

CHAPTER I

Nerves and Muscles: How We Feel and Move

A. V. Hill

1926

✧

The brain speaks the language of electrical signals. It's tempting to focus on how this activity creates the complex workings of the mind – memory, emotions, learning and so on – and easy to forget that some of the most important jobs of the brain involve communicating via these signals and a formidable network of nerves to the entire body. Hill uses some daring experiments to show how this brain–body collaboration is at the heart of all we do.

✧

A day after Hill gives his first Lecture, the newspapers are full of suspiciously unscientific headlines. 'Dead frog brought to life' reads one; 'Dead frog marvel' says another. One report even likens our Lecturer to a magician.

In actual fact, the source of this fascination is not magic but a rather gory experiment involving a nerve and muscle that have been removed from a recently deceased frog. The trick, Hill reveals, is that if kept in the right conditions, a nerve – in this case the sciatic nerve, which runs from the lower back to the feet – can be kept working 'for some time after its previous owner is dead'.

The children are enthralled as Hill shows them the piece of nerve and its connected muscle propped up in a clamp, before stimulating it with an electric current that seems to bring the frog – or at least a part of it – back to life. 'Its nerves and muscles immediately began to move in the liveliest ways', wrote one reporter in the *Birmingham Daily Gazette*. Because nerves and muscles can be kept working after the animal has died, these kinds of experiments have been crucial to much of our understanding about how the body works, Hill says.

The experiment reveals a fundamental property of the nervous system: that it uses electrical signals to communicate. Nerves are the highways that allow the brain to liaise with the rest of the body, sending these electrical messages to and from various muscles and organs at 400 feet per second, faster than an aeroplane, Hill says. 'All that we feel – pain, touch, heat, cold, taste, smell, light, sound – is due to the streams of such nerve waves, started by tiny "microphones" dotted over the outside and scattered throughout the inside of the body. And our replies to these messages, the orders we send to our muscles, are also streams of waves, starting out from the nervous system which lives – well protected – inside our skulls and backbones,' he tells us. (Although Hill doesn't make direct reference to it, the brain and the spinal cord are collectively known as the central nervous system, with the spinal cord relaying messages from around the body up into the brain.)

You could think of this communication system like a telephone network, says Hill. Each nerve is made up of hundreds of long, fine fibres, each about a tenth as thick as a human hair. These fibres carry messages rapidly around the body, a bit like telephone lines. 'The "exchanges" which

7

connect them are the brain and spinal cord.' (A hot flame on our skin, for instance, would send a message to the brain, and in short order another would be sent back from this 'exchange' to the muscles of the hand telling it to pull back from the source of the heat.)

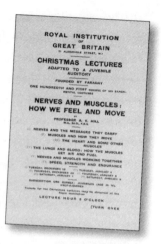

Lecture programme (front cover)

Nerves aren't the only means of communication within the body. We also rely on chemical signals that travel through the blood, but these are much slower, 'like using a postcard instead of a telephone'. These slower signals were probably a precursor to our advanced nervous systems, used by more primitive animals, 'and the nervous system was gradually evolved until it reached its highest efficiency in man'. Another reason why our nervous system is so efficient is that we are hot blooded, Hill explains. All living processes happen more quickly the warmer the animal, which is also the answer to another conundrum – why a tortoise can run faster in the sun than in the shade.

Turning his attention from dead frogs to living children, Hill next enlists the help of his son David for two more spectacular demonstrations. First, proving how electrical signals from the brain cause our muscles to work, he passes a current through David's ulnar nerve, which travels down the arm into the fingers. The effect is dramatic; as one reporter writes in the *Exeter and Plymouth Gazette*, 'his little finger was shown twitching … four or five times as fast as it would be possible for anyone to move the finger'.

And in case there was any lingering doubt about the importance of electricity as the message-bearer to and from the brain to the rest of the body, Hill ends his first Lecture with his most theatrical illustration yet. On stage, David is joined by his younger sister Polly, and their father passes an electric current of 500,000 volts through their bodies, causing showers of violet sparks to fly from their limbs. The audience is gobsmacked. 'All the warnings they had had about avoiding electric shocks were written plain in his hearers' faces, and the youngsters sat with somewhat serious expressions,' several newspapers reported afterwards. 'But eleven-year-old David Hill smiled as he advanced to the table. It was nothing, was what his bearing declared.'

Hill reassures the audience that the experiment is safe because he is using a high-frequency current, which oscillates so fast that any potentially harmful current in the body is instantly reversed. 'Make sure

Polly and David Hill assisting their father during the Lectures with the electric shock demonstration

they are high-frequency currents,' Hill warns as he ends his Lecture to enthusiastic cheers. 'One thousand volts low frequency is sufficient to kill any of us.' Once they realize the experiment is perfectly safe, Hill is mobbed on stage by children keen to try it for themselves, and the press is equally impressed. 'Not all the make-believe magic of pantomime or fairy play could equal the real magic of Professor A. V. Hill's demonstrations', writes one reporter the next day in *The Scotsman*.

Hill returns to the muscles in his second Lecture, as they are the recipients of a large number of these messages from the brain. 'A muscle is a mass of thousands of thin jelly-like living threads,' he says. Each of these threads is attached to a nerve fibre, 'along which it receives the messages to work'. When it receives a message from its nerve, the muscle shortens, or stiffens, Hill explains, because each electrical impulse causes a twitch – a sudden rise then fall in tension. If the signals come close enough together, the twitches can fuse, causing a constant contraction.

After a while, Hill continues, this activity causes the muscles to become tired, so in this respect they are like a battery and need to be recharged. It is David who once again is called upon to demonstrate this idea, in an unusual contest against a dead frog. Just as they respond to signals from the brain, muscles can be made to work artificially in response to an electric shock, and Hill sends a small current through both David's arm and a piece of frog muscle. The muscles begin to twitch, causing a spotlight projected onto a screen to jiggle up and down, so the audience can follow the contest. It is the frog's twitches that begin to wane first, but 'froggie is by no means tired yet,' says Hill, to which David replies: 'Nor am I,' and the audience cheers him on. Eventually, the frog's muscle begins to fail and the light on the screen sinks down to zero. David had to win out, Hill explains, because the frog's muscle has no blood supply to 'recharge it' with fresh oxygen.

This is the job of the heart, 'the most beautiful and important' of the muscles that don't move our limbs, says Hill. No conscious thought is required to keep our heart beating, as we all know, and yet as Hill goes on to show in his next Lecture, it is nonetheless the brain that keeps it ticking.

Two nerves perform an intricate dance to control how fast the heart beats, Hill explains. The vagus nerve sends signals from the brain to slow the heart rate. It is working away all the time as we go about our daily life (especially when we are feeling calm and relaxed). In times of stress or physical activity, however, the sympathetic nervous system takes over, signalling the vagus nerve to quieten down and the heart to beat faster. This process can also kick in when we feel a flood of nerves or emotions. 'Some of us will know how our heart rate rushes up when we are suddenly called upon to make an after-dinner speech,' Hill says.

(Hill was truly ahead of his time, and we are only now realizing just how interconnected the heart and the mind really are. Not only does the brain tell the heart how fast to beat, but internal signals from the body such as our heartbeat also influence our brain. For instance, studies show that people who are more in tune to their heartbeat make better decisions and have heightened emotions, even if they are not aware of it. And those receiving therapy for phobias respond better if the treatment is given in time with their beating heart. It's as if the heart is aware of things before the brain, so some scientists think this internal signalling to the brain could be a kind of gut instinct, giving new meaning to the saying 'go with your heart'.)

Anyone who has ever been startled and felt their pulse rate surge in response will have little doubt about this connection between the brain and the heart, but to prove it Hill demonstrates a fairly new device called a string galvanometer, which made it possible to measure the activity of the heart in real time. Electrical signals given off when the heart beats cause a thin wire to move in sync, and a volunteer's heart beat is projected live in front of the audience – a cutting-edge demonstration at the time.

Polly tries out the string galvanometer

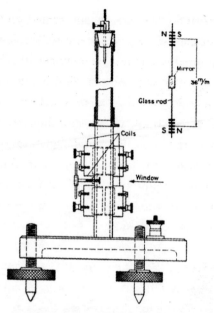

*When a current passes through the galvanometer, magnets
turn a mirror, creating a pulsing beam of light*

This ability to reveal the workings of our nerves
and muscles for all to see could have many uses,
and Hill captures the imagination of the audience as
well as the press when he suggests it might lay bare
our most private emotions – for instance, who we
are in love with.

Even the most stubborn of us cannot hide our
involuntary reflexes from quite simple instruments,

our Lecturer announces. 'If you put a young man in the circuit and read a list of young ladies' names,' he says, 'you would find at some particular name or names he would give an immediate response which would be recorded on the scale. You could get all sorts of secrets out of people in that way.' This idea seems particularly compelling to newspaper reporters. 'Are you in love? If you are, and wish to disguise the fact, you should keep well out of the way of Professor A. V. Hill', writes one in the *Liverpool Echo* the next day. 'For the professor, to whom, as a scientist, not even the most tender of the emotions is sacred, has invented a machine that will reveal the state and object of your affections, however much you try to conceal the fact.'

The demonstration is a source of much concern for another journalist penning a women's column in the *Derby Daily Telegraph*. 'The death-knell has sounded to all those who pride themselves on being able to hide their feelings,' she says, going on to predict that when a device such as Hill's becomes widely available, it will be impossible to disguise the true target of our affections, however hard we try. 'Our questioner might not detect it, but the instrument cannot be deceived. So that's that!'

A. V. Hill (1886–1977)

Going by his initials A. V., Bristol-born Archibald Vivian Hill studied mathematics at Trinity College Cambridge before developing an interest in physiology. In 1920, he became Professor of Physiology at Victoria University of Manchester (now the University of Manchester), before moving to University College London where he remained for the rest of his career. Much of his best-known work focuses on the biochemistry that takes place when muscles undertake work. In 1922, he shared the Nobel Prize in Physiology and Medicine for his work on the production of heat in muscles.

As well as signalling our emotional states, these kinds of automatic reflexes are important in controlling our movements, as Hill goes on to show. We aren't always consciously aware of these signals, but they keep us on our toes, sometimes quite literally. To illustrate this, the audience is shown beautiful slow-motion footage of a famous Russian ballerina, who happens to be Hill's sister-in-law, Lydia Lopokova, in a film made specially for the Lectures. Other footage shows how a black cat is dropped from a height, and in mid-air responds to nerve signals in order to flip over and land on all fours (a demonstration that is repeated live in Colin Blakemore's Lectures on senses; see page 97). 'The cat has only one-fifth of a second to carry out all the complicated movements needed to make him fall on his feet when dropped,' says Hill, emphasizing how rapid, coordinated actions like this and Lopokova's stunning dance moves result from intricate signalling between the brain, our nervous system and our muscles.

You don't have to be a famous dancer (or a feline) to experience this phenomenon, of course. 'In any emergency, like slipping off the step of a bus, the conscious "you" is the very last person to know anything at all about the accident. By the time you've realized you've slipped, all your nerves and muscles have acted, instantaneously, and saved you all it is possible to save you, automatically.' Even a frog that has had its head cut off will continue to scratch things from its back thanks to these automatic signals, Hill adds.

How does the body choreograph these un-conscious feats? 'All these things depend upon the continuous passage of millions of messages to and fro along our nerves, telling us where everything is, and giving orders to our muscles,' says Hill. In its simplest form, the system works when messages come in to the nervous system from our senses along sensory nerves and are sent via the spinal cord to the brain. It then sends instructions back through motor nerves to the muscles, telling them what to do. These 'exchanges' also send messages to the brain to keep the individual informed of what is happening. More complicated reflexes, of course, involve many more signals and muscles.

Bringing his Lectures to a close, Hill imparts to his audience his own sense of wonder and appreciation for his subject at a time when great strides are being made in our understanding of how the body works.

There are few small boys and not many grown men [and presumably girls and women too], who do not want to take machinery apart to see how it works. We cannot do this with our bodies, but there are other ways of finding out about it. We cannot hope yet to understand our living mechanisms fully, but even the little we know already can add delight to physical exertion, and can make us realize the complexity of muscular skill, the nature of strength and endurance; and the effort to understand will help us to appreciate the beauty and wonder of the devices with which our bodies are endowed.

FROM A. V. HILL ...

In 1943, Hill's book based on his Christmas Lectures series, *Living Machinery*, was published. In it, he recalls the experience of being asked to give the talks:

When Sir William Bragg invited me to give these Christmas Lectures, I summoned my family and asked their advice. They had no doubt about an answer, and it was decided that I should accept the invitation. What should I lecture about? Here I got very little help. The only positive suggestion came from David (aged eleven), who, remembering perhaps that these lectures are given to young people shortly after Christmas, a time of good cheer, not only moral but material, proposed that I should lecture on 'How We Taste Things'. It was with regret that

I felt unable to carry out David's suggestion, but I feared that it might be difficult for me to lecture for six whole hours on the subject, and I foresaw that demonstrations with experiments on it might lead to ill-feeling. Were I to use my own family only for experiments on this subject of how to taste things (presumably good things), it might make the rest of my audience jealous and the family sick. If I carried out the experiments on the whole of the audience, it might make the Royal Institution bankrupt.

From the archive …

Writing in the journal *Nature* a month after finishing his Lectures, Hill muses on his experience of speaking to a young audience. It's not an easy task, he says, but many academics – who are prone to overcomplicating things – could benefit from pitching their Lectures at a younger crowd. 'By attempting to make them interesting to a child of thirteen,' he observes, 'they may well succeed in absorbing the attention even of adults comparatively expert in the matter.' Another benefit of talking to

CHAPTER 2

COLOURS AND HOW WE SEE THEM

Hamilton Hartridge

1946

✧

It is just four years since the Christmas Lectures resumed after a wartime hiatus, and Hartridge has chosen a subject he hopes will restore a sense of wonder and awe about the world we live in. We discover how our eyes transform the physical properties of light into information the brain can use to recreate the colourful world around us in our mind's eye. And in the first of several Lectures about human perception, we are shown how things are not always as they seem.

✧

'In this drab postwar world, a world of shortages, restrictions and difficulties … what remains to remind us of the happy past and to give us encouragement for a prosperous future?' Hartridge asks. One answer is colour. 'The rich hues of spring and autumn, the glories of the setting sun, the spectrum of the rainbow. All these are just as perfect as ever they were. The war has not spoiled for us the beauties of nature; rather has it added to our appreciation of them.'

Whether we are admiring the setting sun or a spectacular rainbow, everything we see begins its journey to the brain as light entering the eye, and before we can start to understand this rich experience of colour, we first need to understand something of the physics of light itself.

Our first real insight into how colours are created came from Sir Isaac Newton, who discovered that plain white light is made up of a mixture of coloured rays. Hartridge shows an image of this famous experiment that is featured in a book from the RI's archive, and describes how Newton drilled a small hole in one of his window shutters to allow a narrow beam of sunlight into his darkened room. When the beam hit a glass prism, it was refracted and split into the visible spectrum – all the separate colours of the rainbow – with red at one end and violet at the other.

Hartridge wants to recreate the experiment in the RI, but there's a snag. 'Now, the Christmas Lectures are given at the end of the year, when sunlight is notoriously unreliable,' he points out. Instead, an artificial beam of light is shone dramatically from the back of the Lecture Theatre over the heads of his audience. When it hits a large glass prism, positioned on a pedestal in the middle of the stage, just like in Newton's room it is split into a splendid colour spectrum, which is projected like a three-foot rainbow on a lantern screen.

A diagram from Hartridge's book depicting the re-creation of Newton's experiment during his Lectures

Newton was aware only of these visible rays, but Hartridge explains that in the last century scientists have discovered that there are other parts of the electromagnetic spectrum that aren't, under normal circumstances, visible to the human eye. 'Thus the visible rays that we call "light" form only a small part of the whole spectrum,' (although technology can reveal this invisible world, as Hartridge shows his audience with a hidden infrared camera).

The reason why only this part of the spectrum is visible to us has to do with the design of the eye. The full spectrum is composed of different wavelengths

A photograph of the Lecture audience taken with a hidden infrared camera

of light, and most of these wavelengths can't be detected by our eyes. Radio waves, for instance, cannot be absorbed by the retina, and heat waves can't make it through the gel-like fluids inside the eye. One exception, says Hartridge, is people who have had their cornea removed during cataract surgery. The cornea normally blocks much of the ultraviolet light hitting the eye, so these patients can be left with superhuman vision – able to see into the ultraviolet wavelengths.

The colours of the spectrum, too, each have a characteristic wavelength, which is vital to how we see them. Most of the colours we experience are the result of some of the constituents of white light being removed, and others being reflected for the eye to see, explains Hartridge. As an example, 'we might mention the green colour of grass, which owes its properties to the fact that chlorophyll, while absorbing the blue-violet and the orange-red rays, reflects the green rays strongly'. But before we can perceive the greenness of the grass or any other colour in our surroundings, the eyes need to turn these light waves into a signal that the brain can make use of.

Light travelling into the eye is focused onto the retina, a 'hollow cup' lining the inside of the eyeball,

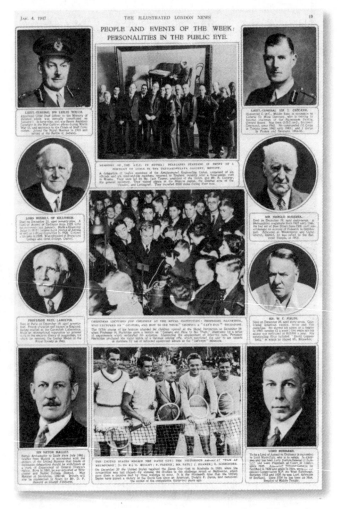

*Hartridge's Lectures take centre stage in a roundup of the week
in the* Illustrated London News

says Hartridge, and this is where the action happens. The lens system of the eye produces sharply focused images of external objects, after which 'it is the function of the retina to convert these images into nerve impulses, and then it is the function of the brain to utilize these nerve impulses for the purposes of sensation, so that we see external objects'.

The retina is lined with millions of light-detecting cells called rods and cones (named after their shapes), and it is these that turn incoming light into signals to be processed by the brain. (In fact, more than half of the sensory receptors in the entire body are found in the eyes.) The rods are much more sensitive than the cones and enable us to see in dim light, whereas the cones work in bright light and give us our colour vision.

These electrical signals are then sent to the brain via the optic nerve, and Hartridge describes how this gives rise to a strange phenomenon. All the nerve fibres carrying signals out of the back of the retina bundle together to form the base of the optic nerve, and to make room for this bundle there is one spot on the retina where there are no light receptors at all. 'In consequence, this particular part of the eyeball is blind,' Hartridge declares. We don't tend to notice this blind spot in daily life, but there's an easy way to prove it's there with nothing more than a paper and pencil.

Two small crosses are drawn on the paper two inches apart, and Hartridge then shows us how to make one of them disappear in front of our eyes. The observer must cover their right eye and look at one of the crosses with their left, before rotating the paper so that the other cross is now on the left-hand side of the first. All the while keeping the left eye fixed on the right-hand cross, the paper must be brought slowly towards the eye. When it is about nine inches away, the left-hand cross will suddenly disappear. 'This disappearance is due to the fact that the image of the left-hand cross coincides with the blind-spot,' Hartridge explains. (For more blind-spot tricks, see Colin Blakemore's Lectures, page 97.)

Lecture programme
(front cover)

Hartridge also describes another part of the eyeball, which is densely packed with cones; the *fovea centralis*. 'This central hollow is the part of the retina which gives the most acute vision for fine detail,' he says (this is the level of detail we would need for reading or driving. In fact, as you move your eyes to read this, you are placing the words in your *fovea*).

Concerning our experience of seeing colours, Hartridge describes how we owe much of our understanding to two men, John Dalton and Thomas Young. Over a hundred years before the Lectures, Young had come up with the trichromatic theory of colour vision, the idea that we have three types of receptor in the eye responsible for the perception of colour, each sensitive to a certain range of visible light – one receptor for red rays, another for blue and a third for yellow. 'He chose red, yellow and blue because he knew that painters, by using these three primary colours, find that it is possible to match practically all other colours,' Hartridge explains (the theory was later updated to red, green and blue cones).

'Now let us deal with our other celebrity,' he continues. 'John Dalton was famous not only as a chemist, but also as the first person to give a scientific description to the curious and interesting kind of colour-blindness which we now call "dichromatism".' We hear how Dalton was seriously disadvantaged when picking cherries as a child in the orchard, because the fruit and the leaves both appeared to be the same colour. Thinking that other boys experienced the same thing, it wasn't until years later, when he wore a red coat to a funeral (he thought the coat was grey) that 'the exclamations of the other mourners drew his attention to his visual defect'. These might just be amusing anecdotes, says Hartridge, but either way Dalton went on to explain what was wrong – while he had green and blue receptors, he had none for red.

Something that was poorly understood at the time of these Lectures was exactly how cones tell the brain which colours we are looking at, a fact Hartridge is happy to admit. 'It would be a very great mistake to suppose that the problem of colour vision is one which has been completely solved,' he says. According to Young, the retina contains light-sensitive chemicals that break down when light falls on them. 'The breakdown caused by red rays differs essentially from that produced by green rays or blue rays,' Hartridge explains, resulting in three different breakdown products that will be present in different amounts depending on the colours we are looking at. It's then the job of the cones to act as very sensitive detectors, each type of cone sensing the presence of one of these breakdown products.

Hamilton Hartridge (1886–1976)

Making a precarious entrance into the world, Hartridge was born in Stamford Hill, London, when two giant traction engines passed by his house and shook the ceiling so hard that it fell onto his pregnant mother. The accident caused her to go into labour prematurely, and the baby had slim chances of survival. But Hartridge lived to the age of eighty-nine and became an acclaimed eye physiologist. He studied at King's College Cambridge, and later became Professor of Physiology at St Bartholomew's Hospital Medical School. He was elected a Fellow of the Royal Society in 1926. Hartridge became best known not only for his work on the physiology of the eye and colour vision perception, but also as an ingenious experimenter, a skill that made his Christmas Lectures a treat to watch.

Another way to understand it is to compare the cone receptors on the retina to taste buds on the tongue, Hartridge suggests. Imagine that we could make a substance that was tasteless when placed on the tongue, but 'under the action of light the chemical substance in question is broken down so as to liberate a sweet substance like saccharine'. Soon we would begin to associate opening our mouths with a sweet sensation, he says. What's more, in the dark there would be no effect, but it would taste especially sweet if we opened our mouths near a window. 'We should then quickly correlate the intensity of the sweetness with the intensity of the light, and the tips of our tongues would temporarily have become light detectors.'

Taking the idea further, if we had a substance that responded to the shortest wavelengths of light, one that produced a different taste for the middle of the spectrum and another for the longest, then 'after a little practice we would be able to say with certainty what is the colour of the light that is falling on them'. (We now know that this thought experiment was almost correct. The light-sensitive molecules that he describes are called photopigments, but they are present in the rods and cones themselves. Each of the photopigments in the three different types of cone cell responds optimally to different wavelengths of light, and is therefore more sensitive to the wavelengths that represent red, green or blue.)

Having shown how the physical properties of colours in the world around us are picked up by the eye, our Lecturer now reveals how this system can be deceived.

The penultimate Lecture begins with a spectacular and mysterious performance. Once the audience are settled in their seats, a curtain is drawn back to reveal a shapeless grey object lying on a platform. As music starts to fill the auditorium, the shape slowly comes to life, extending first a bat-like wing, then standing rigidly, before stumbling down to the theatre floor. This 'repellent-looking object', as Hartridge calls it, jerks about stiffly, but as the music gathers pace it begins to dash in one direction and then the other, its drab body and wings slowly transforming into the vivid hues of a magnificent butterfly. The insect flutters around in the brilliant light and then, as the music dies down, so the butterfly fades once again to the sound of enthusiastic applause from the audience.

The butterfly dance, which was performed by Miss Lewis, the granddaughter of physicist Alexander Rankine, who himself gave the Christmas Lectures in 1932, is the embodiment of a striking illusion of colour – the subject of this Lecture.

There are three types of colour illusion, according to Hartridge, and this is an example of the first; when colours are present but we don't see them for some reason. We discover that the butterfly turns from dull to brilliant colour in front of our eyes thanks to a trick of the light. At the start of the performance, the auditorium was illuminated with sodium lamps, which emit only yellow rays and, as a result, yellow objects show up very brightly – other colours are masked and appear dark grey or black. As the butterfly emerged, ordinary light was slowly added. Finally a spotlight on the dancing butterfly brought to life all its glorious colours. Another, more familiar example of this illusion is apparent when we sit by the light of glowing coals. 'By such a light, red objects appear bright, and green and blue objects appear dark,' Hartridge points out.

Other times, we see colours where there are none – instead, they are conjured up by the brain itself. Some of the best-known examples of this were discovered by a mysterious individual who was known at the time simply as Benham. 'It has been possible to find very little information about this man. His antecedents, the date of his birth, even his Christian name, cannot be traced; but "Benham's top" will be known, it is hoped, for all of time.' (We now know much more about this character; Charles Benham was a British journalist and keen amateur scientist.) Benham drew a black-and-white pattern on a disc and showed that if it is slowly rotated like a spinning top, streaks of colour seem to appear.

'Some of the illusions which he discovered by means of his top are very striking and very baffling,' says Hartridge. (To this day, the cause of this illusion continues to elude scientists, but one explanation is to do with the way the cones work in the retina. All types of cone should respond to the white part of the disc, but because the three types respond to incoming light at different speeds, the confusion causes colour to be perceived instead.)

More phantom colours come in the form of simultaneous contrast illusions. The audience is shown a piece of card, half of which is blue-green and the other half pale pink, and in the middle of each half lies a ring-shaped piece of card of the contrasting colour – a blue-green ring on the pink side and vice versa. The onlookers are asked to confirm that this is indeed what they are all seeing, but to their surprise when the discs are removed from their backgrounds, they are both revealed to be the exact same grey colour. It turns out that the way our brain perceives colours is also down to the context of the other colours surrounding them, turning grey into pink and blue-green at the same time.

Anyone who has ever looked at a bright light, then closed their eyes, will be familiar with our Lecturer's next illusion. 'After a few moments the image of the light will repeat itself over and over again, particularly if the eyes are kept as still as possible,' he says. Known as an after-image, the effect also happens with colours. If, after fixing the eyes on a coloured cross on a white piece of card, we then look at a blank card, an after-image of the cross will appear on the blank sheet. The only difference is that the cross will have changed colours – the after-image will be a complementary colour to the original. (We still don't know for definite what causes these colourful after-images and Hartridge does not attempt to explain them, but a possible explanation is to do with the signals sent to the brain from the cones in the retina. If we look at one source of coloured light for too long, the photopigments become depleted and the signals to the brain weaken. If we then look at a bright white image – such as a plain piece of card – all the cones should be stimulated, but if the exhausted stores of photopigment have not yet replenished, this particular colour is underrepresented and we see its complementary colour instead. The reason this doesn't happen normally is that the eyes are constantly on the move, as we will see for ourselves in Bruce Hood's Lectures in Chapter 9, so we never fixate on one colour for too long.)

As Hartridge draws his Lectures to a close, there is little doubt that he has succeeded in his aim to

CHAPTER 3

THE MIND AT WORK AND AT PLAY

Sir Frederic Bartlett

1948

✧

Some of the biggest mysteries of science lie very close to home, inside our own heads. In the first ever Christmas Lecture series on psychology given at the RI, Bartlett invites the audience to offer up their own psyches as the test subjects for his experiments, which often involve tricky puzzles and baffling illusions. Through these, he ambitiously sets out to probe some of the biggest questions about the human mind, including how memory works and how we think; subjects that still challenge scientists to this day.

✧

Before Bartlett begins his Lectures, he offers some advice to his young audience: 'The best way to take this course of Lectures will be to treat it as a kind of exciting adventure in which we may make new discoveries, or the beginnings of discoveries, at any time.' With the subject being psychology, Bartlett promises that the audience themselves will become the guinea pigs for many of the experiments, and this requires a particular code of conduct. 'Experiments with human beings are different in important ways from experiments with inanimate objects,' he explains. In particular, Bartlett cautions them not to discuss any of the experiments while they are in progress, as 'this will almost certainly influence the results in ways which, for our purpose, are undesirable'.

Lecture programme
(front cover)

During his first Lecture, Bartlett draws attention to the enigmatic behaviour of the human mind by setting the audience a number of tests. He tells them,

'Everybody must have discovered that there are many things that it is perfectly easy to do in one way, but far less easy to do in another way.' One of these is judging distances. As we go about our daily lives, we don't even notice how accurately we do this, and yet we do it all the time, whether eating or drinking or playing ball games. The eyes size up the distance and send a message to the brain, which then communicates with the muscles, and the body does what is required. And yet as soon as we consciously try to put a number to the distance, we become horribly inaccurate.

To prove this, our Lecturer sets his young audience some challenges. In one, a photograph of a canal tunnel is projected onto a screen and they are asked to guess its length. There is huge variation in the answers, with most guessing the tunnel is well under a mile long and the highest answer coming in at thirteen miles. As an article in the *Daily Herald* reports the next day, Bartlett is astonished when one boy guesses exactly the right answer (four miles), until the boy clarifies, 'I've seen the picture before in a book.'

It turns out we are particularly bad at estimating large distances, and the problem isn't reserved for sight, but 'anything else that the senses can tell us about,' says Bartlett, including the brightness of lights, the speed of movement or the loudness of sounds. The trick lies in having a point of reference, which is why all measuring instruments, from rulers to dials, have some kind of fixed values on them. 'The senses and the mind can get along very well with measurement, if we provide some kind of fixed standard for comparison,' Bartlett explains.

Our minds can also let us down when we become tired. 'Everybody knows that if we have a long continuous spell of activity we tend to get tired, whether at work or at play, and to do less well than

Bartlett tests his audience

we did at the beginning,' says Bartlett. In particular, our Lecturer is interested in what happens when people have to perform a skilled action for long periods of time.

During his career, the Air Force asked Bartlett to investigate the effects of fatigue on fighter pilots. To find out, he built an experimental model of an aeroplane cockpit in his laboratory in Cambridge. In the safety of the lab, the set-up would allow him and his colleagues to get pilots to fly for dangerously long periods, while being given navigational instructions just as they might have been if they were really taking to the skies. 'It seemed certain that when the pilot had to make a very long flight of several hours his skill suffered.'

But as Bartlett and his colleagues discovered, this doesn't always have to be the case. There is a trick everyone can use to keep the mind sharp even after long periods of skilled work and hold the effects of fatigue at bay. The secret is to regularly check in on how you are doing, explains Bartlett. He describes one experiment in which students had to read for hours on end. Unsurprisingly, they tended to make mistakes and skip over parts of the text after a long period. But those who were regularly given comprehension tests as they read didn't seem to suffer any of these effects of fatigue. The same was true of Bartlett's pilots in the laboratory. When they used the dials and instruments provided to check their performance at regular intervals, they didn't make any mistakes or show any signs of fatigue at all. 'One pilot, for example, continued without a break for twelve hours, being fed while he worked, and remained as good at the end as he was at the beginning,' Bartlett recalls. So simply taking stock of how you are performing every now and then can stave off the effects of physical and mental fatigue, Bartlett explains, demonstrating just how strong the power of the mind is over the actions performed by the body.

Bartlett then moves on to the thing that most of us consider to be the 'jobs of the mind itself' – perception. 'For it is through some form or another of this that we learn whatever we know about the world in which we live,' he says.

One of the mysterious things about perception is that some kinds of objects seem to stand out much more than others. To demonstrate, Bartlett shows images of a piece of text with either the top half or the bottom half of all the words missing.

A.

When any practised reader runs his eyes rapidly along the lines of print, is it true to say that all parts of the letters or words read are equally important, or are there perhaps some parts which make a stronger impression than others? Most readers would probably be inclined to say that all parts of the shapes which they interpret have about the same influence.

B.

But here is an experiment which may show that he is wrong. For it usually takes longer to read words when only the bottom halves of the letters are seen than it does to read the same number of words when only the top halves are represented. In fact the upper halves of letters make more impression, or carry more meaning than their bottom halves.

The reading experiment shown in Bartlett's book
based on the Lectures

It is immediately clear that it's much easier to read text when you can see just the top of the words. Part of the reason for this is the way the Roman (or Latin) alphabet is formed. For every letter that projects below the line, seven project above it. But other experiments show there is something more to it, as Bartlett explains. 'People do in fact pay more attention to the upper parts of nearly all kinds of visual display.' In fact, he says, whatever the object, people are much more likely to observe it correctly if it is visible in the upper left of our field of vision (although more recent experiments suggest this isn't always the case, and it depends what sort of thing we are looking at).

There are other ways in which the brain seems pre-programmed to notice specific things over others. Bartlett shows his audience slides containing two rows of hieroglyphic-like symbols, and asks them to write down anything about the two rows that is of particular interest. He then does the same thing with a different set of symbols. In his first example, only one symbol was the same in both lines. In the second set, just one of the symbols in each row was different. A hundred and ninety-five members of the audience submitted an answer. Only eleven noted the point of difference in the first set, but when it came to spotting the similarity in the second set, the results were worse – remarkably, only four people got the answer right.

This illustrates an important point about the workings of the human mind, says Bartlett. We have an innate ability to spot differences over things that are alike (although Bartlett doesn't go into why this might be, it makes sense from an evolutionary perspective because it should have helped our ancestors spot any changes in our environment that could be dangerous, such as a predator).

But the brain is unreliable in all sorts of other strange ways too, and Bartlett uses a special kind of visual illusion to make his point. Showing an image of a square within a larger square, with the corners joined up to look a bit like a lampshade, Bartlett introduces what are known as 'reversible figures'.

Does the square in the square look closer or
further away than the larger square?

These are designed to be ambiguous, creating two equally likely representations of the object (we will discover more of these during Richard Gregory's Lectures; see Chapter 4). As a result, the brain becomes unable to process just one, fixed interpretation of the picture or object. The effect is a mind-boggling experience, because the picture might look like one thing in one moment and then suddenly flip into looking like something else. While we're looking at it, 'it jigs about from one way to another and back again,' explains Bartlett. That's particularly important; the fact that even one person can see something as two different objects at any one time suggests there's no such thing as 'pure' observation.

Bartlett ends this Lecture with perhaps one of the most famous examples of a reversible figure (who we shall meet again in other Lectures) – a young woman turning her head away. Or is it an old woman wearing a headscarf? These kinds of pictures 'raise some very interesting questions and must be further studied,' Bartlett concludes. (Indeed, psychologists today are still debating what causes the brain to fall for these illusions, and it is an enigmatic property of perception that will be of interest to several of our Lecturers.)

Best known for his discoveries about memory, this is the subject of Bartlett's next Lecture. 'Everything we do involves remembering in one form or another,' he begins. And memories also influence the way we see the world. 'When the mind observes, always some of our report is based upon what we ourselves bring with us to the task,' he says. In one ingeniously simple experiment, Bartlett allows his audience the briefest of glances at some slightly muddled phrases, such as 'The Royal Intuition', or 'fish and chops'. The young crowd must then write down on a piece of card the phrase they have just seen. Of 140 cards returned, five wrote 'The Royal Intuition' (which would have been correct) whereas a staggering 103 noted down the more familiar 'The Royal Institution'. Twenty-eight said 'fish and chops,' whereas ninety-seven erroneously corrected it to 'chips'. As Bartlett puts it: 'Familiar and remembered forms are obviously overpowering the immediate work of the eyes.'

So how good are our memories? German psychologist Hermann Ebbinghaus was the first to devise a simple memory test in the 1880s, in which people had to remember lists of made-up words. He discovered that after trying to learn something, people forget an awful lot during the first couple of days. But after that, forgetting seems to slow down and not much more is lost. Ebbinghaus called this the 'curve of forgetting'. As a result, 'cramming the memory is, in fact, hardly ever, except by good luck or accident, a profitable thing to do,' Bartlett warns his young audience.

Bartlett uses the analogy of building a bridge to explain another facet of memory; that we are much better at remembering things at the beginning and end of a list, and more likely to forget the items in the middle. 'When the mind is building up material to be remembered, it often seems to work like people who are building a bridge across a river and who begin on the two banks and proceed towards the middle,' he says. So when trying to remember particularly tricky items on a list, it's better to put them in these privileged positions. This also helps explain a 'difficulty that bothers a lot of folks, especially when they are getting oldish,' Bartlett says, which is the tendency to remember only the initial letter of someone's name.

Quite ahead of his time, Bartlett also muses on the relationship between sleep and memory, with experiments showing that 'sleep does arrest the ordinary process of forgetting', and so we may be advised to learn anything we want to remember before we doze off. (We now know that sleep is vital for strengthening new memories. During this time, the brain sorts newly acquired memories, moving some into long-term storage. It's also while we sleep that the emotional components of memories are processed by the brain.)

Such tips would likely have been of use to the school-aged members of the audience facing tests and exams, but in everyday adult life most of us don't need to recall information word for word. In fact, one of Bartlett's most famous discoveries was the idea that memories aren't a direct record, or a snapshot of something we have seen, with gaps where we have forgotten things, but instead are shaped by our experiences of the past.

To explore the idea, he recreates one of his most renowned experiments. Several volunteers are selected from the audience and all but one are sent out of the room. A large picture is then displayed to the Lecture Theatre and the one remaining volunteer. A second person is soon brought back into the room, but cannot see the picture, while the first person is asked to describe it to them. A third volunteer is then allowed back in, and, still without seeing the image, the second person must describe the picture to the third, and so on.

By turning this game into an experiment and studying the reports and how they change with each person's description, it's possible to work out what kind of information is most easily remembered and what is forgotten. Having carried out this test numerous times in the past, Bartlett has found that the same sorts of details tend to be omitted or changed as the game goes on. For instance, the relative positions of objects are easily forgotten, as are colours, titles and names, and strange details will often be replaced by those more fitting with everyday experience. 'This is a way in which rumours spread, in which opinions may be formed, but in which all the time people's memories claim, and appear, to be at work.' The same sorts of changes will happen to our individual memories too, Bartlett says. However hard we may try to remember something accurately, 'the custom of everyday life will be too strong for us, and changes will creep in, though we may believe we have made no change whatsoever'.

Sir Frederic Bartlett (1886–1969)

Born in Gloucester, Bartlett studied philosophy, as well as ethics and sociology, before moving to Cambridge University and into the field of psychology. Best known for his studies on memory, he was one of the forerunners in the field of cognitive psychology and became the first professor of experimental psychology at Cambridge. As a child, Bartlett suffered from pleurisy and as a result was unable to participate in the First World War. Even so, much of his research was concerned with the military, training, and how the body adapts to new situations. In recognition of this work and his services to the Royal Air Force, Bartlett was knighted the same year he gave the Christmas Lectures.

As his fifth Lecture draws to a close, Bartlett considers one of the biggest mysteries concerning memories: where they are stored in the brain. This is something which is 'incredibly difficult to understand', he notes (it's a problem neuroscientists are still grappling with today, although it is now widely considered the case that memories are stored in the connections between neurons in the brain, as Susan Greenfield discusses in her Lectures, see Chapter 7). Also ahead of the thinking at the time, Bartlett points out that rather than being about the past, remembering is a tool that helps us use what we learn in one situation to deal with other situations in the future. 'We remember things that have happened in one set of circumstances to help us solve problems that arise in a different set.'

Next, Bartlett turns his attention to 'perhaps one of the most important of all the problems' of his Lectures: 'What really happens when we think?' One crucial component of thinking is intelligence, he says, 'because every intelligent person is supposed to be a person who can think if the occasion arises'.

Ebbinghaus, who pioneered memory testing, also laid the groundwork for the first intelligence tests, by devising an exercise in which schoolchildren had to fill in missing words or phrases from fables. Since then, 'inventing intelligence tests has almost achieved the rank of a sport,' says Bartlett, but tellingly many such tests also involved some sort of gap-filling exercise. This makes sense, Bartlett explains, given that most of the time our brain has to fill in gaps in the information provided by the senses. As he neatly sums up, 'We fill up the gaps without knowing there were any.' This seems to Bartlett to be the essence of how the mind works, and a crucial aspect of thinking. (Although these ideas would now be considered a little simplistic, it is true that the brain is constantly filling in gaps, especially when it comes to perception, and in recent years theories similar to Bartlett's have grown in popularity – most notably the Bayesian brain hypothesis, which suggests that the brain constantly makes probabilistic predictions to fill in gaps.)

There are several ways the mind thinks by filling in gaps. Sometimes doing so requires a sequence of logical steps, but there are some types of problem that seem to defy logic and instead can only be solved by a flash of inspiration – what we might call 'intuition' or 'insight'.

Bartlett provides an example in the 'horse and rider puzzle'. The image overleaf shows two horses drawn back to back on one sheet of paper. On another we can see two riders, one upside down. The trick is to somehow place the picture of the riders

over that of the horses, 'in such a way that there will be a rider astride upon each horse in the proper position,' Bartlett says. At first this seems impossible, but the ingenious solution is that the front legs of one horse belong to the back legs of the other.

This sort of problem requires a 'radical' change to the way we approach it, which usually only happens with 'laborious trial and error or by the sudden flash of insights,' our Lecturer explains. 'Many of the world's most brilliant inventions do appear to have been made in this intuitive manner.'

Bartlett leaves his audience with a final question; 'Can minds be trained to think?' We have seen that there are errors to which the mind seems particularly prone, and understanding these can be helpful, he says. But there is one vital ingredient for a good thinker that is hard to pin down, 'something for which we have no other word than "wisdom",' Bartlett muses. Being wise helps a thinker to decide which clues are worth exploring and those 'whose exploration will merely lead to a wilderness of trouble'. And while wisdom is a 'fruit' that can be acquired through experience, it isn't guaranteed, Bartlett points out with an air of mystery. 'If only we could discover for certain the differences between those who, being given about the same opportunities, acquire wisdom and those who do not, perhaps we could say whether we could plan with success to produce the wise thinker. As it is, there is nothing for it but to admit that nobody knows.'

CHAPTER 4

THE INTELLIGENT EYE

Richard L. Gregory

1967

Vision might seem simple – our eyes send pictures to the brain, which makes us aware of them. But the experience of seeing is much more than that, and in these Lectures Gregory shows us just how much of what we see really comes from the brain, not the eye. Renowned for his work with optical illusions, Gregory uses some mind-boggling examples to expose the brain in action. It's an illuminating journey of discovery that starts with ancient water-dwelling creatures before taking us to the moon and beyond.

A familiar analogy kicks off this Lecture series: that the eye is like a camera. But it's not one our Lecturer is fond of. For while eyes and cameras both capture images, a camera cannot actually *see*. 'To see there must be a brain to accept information from images and make sense of it. The theme of these Lectures is how the camera-eye and the computer-brain give the miracle of sight.'

Our relationship with reality – the everyday experience of external objects – is a subject that 'has fascinated and puzzled philosophers since the start of human thought,' he says. But it is only in recent years that we have started to gain a true understanding of how the brain interprets information from the eyes to create that experience.

Before we get to that, however, there's a thorny problem to solve, which is the subject of Gregory's first Lecture. 'What use is an eye without a brain to accept its information? What use is a "visual" brain without an eye?' Gregory asks. In other words, what came first: eye or brain?

Working models of the eye are brought on to help demonstrate how this sense first developed, and Gregory invites us to imagine an early ancestor, a sea-dwelling creature with a primitive nervous system

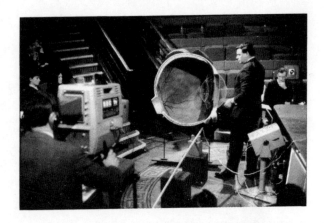

Gregory describes how the eye evolved

conveying just the sense of touch, that acted like a simple reflex in response to the world around it.

Even if touch was originally the master sense to the sea creature, its skin was probably also sensitive to light and dark patterns, Gregory suspects, as these would give useful warning of impending danger. With time, these handy light receptors on the skin would have become concentrated into specific 'eye pits'. A lens then formed over the top as a window to prevent the eye pits from getting blocked by tiny particles floating in the waters that these animals called home. Gradually, these windows would have thickened, intensifying the light hitting the eye pits until the whole thing transformed into an image-forming eye, in which the images were then picked up by the primitive nervous system.

For some animals, sight remains relatively simple, and Gregory 'uses a minute water insect to explain the wonders of sight', according to a report in the *Liverpool Echo* on 28 December 1967. In fact, it's not an insect but a crustacean and we hear how Gregory's fascination with the development of the eye led him on an expedition to Italy to try to find this creature fabled to have a most curious visual system. Having sifted through gallons of water from the Bay of Naples, Gregory did find the animal, called Copilia, and was able to confirm rumours that its bizarre eye has just one channel to the brain. 'Eyes such as our own transmit information by a million channels,' he explains, 'but images can be transmitted – as in television – by "scanning" with a single channel.'

For other animals, however, the ability to see had a much more profound impact on the brain, Gregory says. Exploring the world through touch is a precarious way to live – imagine you had to poke a predator just to find out it was there! So vision conferred a huge advantage: the ability to see out into the distance, to spot danger coming. And to make sense of these images required much smarter brains. 'As we shall see, eyes require intelligence to identify and locate objects ... but intelligent brains could hardly have developed without eyes.' Indeed, Gregory says, 'it is not too much to say that the eyes freed the nervous system from the tyranny of reflexes, leading ... ultimately to abstract thinking.'

Having solved the problem of how our eyes and brains developed together, Gregory next turns his attention to another conundrum. Are we born with the ability to make sense of what we see, or is it something we have to learn? Babies can't tell us how they see the world, of course, but we can get some clues from simple experiments. Babies spend longer looking at faces than images that have all the same features as a face, but jumbled up, suggesting an in-built facial recognition system.

Gregory has another clever way to probe this question, and he describes his work with a man who became blind aged ten months but had his sight restored after an operation as an adult, over fifty years later. Gregory and his colleagues wanted to find out what his perception of the world was like as he rediscovered it, as if for the first time.

Richard Gregory (1923–2010)

London-born Gregory left school at seventeen to join the RAF. In 1947, he went to Cambridge University on a scholarship from the RAF, where he was taught cognitive psychology by fellow Christmas Lecturer Frederic Bartlett. Gregory went on to become an eminent psychologist, his work principally concerned with perception and, later, artificial intelligence. A celebrated communicator of science, he was well known for his work on optical illusions, and wrote several popular science books. At the time of giving these Christmas Lectures he had just founded the pioneering Department for Perception and Machine Intelligence at the University of Edinburgh.

The patient, known by his initials SB, longed to see again, Gregory recalls. 'But though the operation was a success, the story ends in tragedy.' At first, SB was enchanted with his restored sense, but soon became disillusioned. While he could recognize things that he had learned to 'see' through touch, SB struggled with items he had not been able to feel before. For instance, when drawing a bus, he would leave out the details he had never touched, such as the front of the vehicle. He also found it hard to approximate distances, and while he had previously been confident crossing the road, he was now terrified by traffic. He found the world drab and became depressed, often preferring to sit in the dark. He died a few years later.

This sad tale revealed something important about perception. Gregory's work showed that the images reaching the retina were the same for SB as for anyone else, but somehow his brain struggled to make sense of the information. 'Perception is a kind of problem solving, a skill that has to be learned,' Gregory concludes.

In his next Lecture, Gregory's focus turns to what happens when this perceptual problem-solving system goes wrong. 'When it comes up with a wrong answer, we suffer a visual illusion.'

'Illusions can be entertaining and useful, as well as dangerous,' he says. 'In this Lecture we will look at many kinds of illusions and play games with them. Just as we get to know our friends by playing with them, so we can get to know science through games.' First we are shown examples of op art (optical art), a kind of abstract art that uses illusions and 'plays games with the brain,' as Gregory put it. We see pictures by op artists Victor Vasarely and Bridget Riley, who use black-and-white patterns to give the erroneous impression that the image is shifting and shimmering. What causes these effects is somewhat of a mystery, although Gregory suspects it has to do with an overloading of the brain's visual-processing systems by pushing them to their limits.

'Much of art is an illusion,' Gregory points out, but illusions can be much more than a visual treat. 'Illusions may appear trivial,' he says, introducing his next Lecture, 'but so did the early experiments with rubbed amber and pith balls, which led to atomic energy and understanding of the energy of the stars. If illusions can tell us something of how the brain handles information they become tools for research.' In other words, if we can understand why the brain is confused by even simple shapes, 'this leads us to what happens in the brain, all day long, while we are looking at things.'

As we saw in Hartridge's 1946 Lectures (see page 23), light is just energy hitting the eye, so how do we turn that into objects that mean something to us? For instance, a table could be any number of shapes, colours and sizes, and yet we seem to know instinctively what is and isn't a table. This is what Gregory means when he says that perception is about problem solving. The brain often has limited information to work with, and needs to turn that into useful concepts.

Gregory's explanations of how the brain does this are perhaps some of his most important contributions to psychology, and it is these ideas that he talks to his audience about now, with the help of some striking illusions. We hear how, rather than simply seeing the world around us, the brain probably contains a kind of reference library of past experiences that it uses each time we see something. It can then compare any information reaching the eye with this stored knowledge and make a hypothesis about what it is seeing. For instance, we can attribute meaning to a smile because of past knowledge about what that facial expression means. (Incidentally, SB was unable to understand facial expressions once his vision was restored. Having never seen a smile before, he had no stored 'knowledge' about its social meaning.)

Gregory turns to a famous illusion to help prove his point. A giant red wireframe cube hangs from the ceiling; it's a Necker cube, a kind of illusion known as an ambiguous or reversible figure. As Bartlett described in his Lectures (see Chapter 3), when we look at these shapes, they seem to change in front of our very eyes. At first, one face of the cube is in the foreground and then the other. The information reaching the retina is constant, Gregory explains, but the perception of it changes from instant to instant as one hypothesis is tested, and then the other. 'Each is entertained in turn, but none is allowed to stay because none is better than the others.'

To explore this idea further, Gregory shows us a peculiar-looking wooden triangle on the Lecture desk. It is made of solid wood, but each of the corners appear to be joined at right  angles, which we know cannot be physically possible. This is an example of an 'impossible object', Gregory explains. 'The eye roves

Gregory demonstrates the impossible triangle illusion

around trying to get a sense of them, but never finds a solution because there is none.'

As the television audience at home marvels at this paradoxical sight, some of the children in the Lecture Theatre will have already glimpsed the solution. This object is not a triangle at all; the three pieces of wood do not connect up, but only appear to do so from a particular camera angle (we see something similar with the Ames room, in Bruce Hood's 2011 Lectures; see page 157). Objects such as these further show the brain as a tester of hypotheses. Having never seen such a strange object before, the brain can't possibly guess that the triangle is really three pieces of wood joined at jaunty angles, so it settles for another solution even if we know it to be impossible. 'The true solution … is an extremely unlikely solution to the problem,' Gregory says, adding that it is especially interesting that even when we know the correct answer, we still struggle not to see the triangle in its impossible form. 'Though visual perception involves problem solving, evidently it does not follow that when we know the solution intellectually we will necessarily see it correctly.'

*The young audience crowd around the Lecture Theatre desk
at the end of one of Gregory's Lectures*

In another illusion, the Kanizsa triangle, a bright
white triangle appears where there is none (see below),
again showing how the brain uses prior experience –
in this case, the understanding that one object can hide
another – to jump to conclusions rather than see what
is really there. We also return
to an illusion from Hartridge's
Lectures, and Gregory shows
how Benham's top, a black-and-
white patterned disc, when spun,
turns into colour in front of our
eyes (see page 37).

Even if the brain gets things wrong sometimes – as in the case of these illusions – being able to draw on past experiences in this way is incredibly useful, Gregory explains. By doing so the brain becomes a prediction machine, taking limited sensory information to build a new picture of what is likely to happen in the future.

Having shown that illusions can make handy research tools, we now see how they can be applied to a very practical purpose. Gregory is giving his Lectures just two years before man would walk on the moon and he has been employed by the US Air Force to try and work out how visual illusions might affect astronauts in the vacuum of space. Speculating that man will need to be sent into space to report back on the moon and the planets, we need to know how reliable their eyes and brains are in these foreign lands, he says. Our eyes have evolved step by step to work in the environment we live in. In the dark vastness of space, without much by way of a reference point, strange illusions could also present grave dangers to astronauts.

For instance, we know that isolation plays tricks on the mind; when deprived of sensory information

Gregory discusses human perception in space

even for short periods people tend to hallucinate. It's as if the sensory system needs constant updates or it 'goes off on its own', Gregory explains.

From experiments in his own laboratory, Gregory describes some of the tricks of the mind that could occur if we needed to build a space station in orbit (it is still a good thirty years before work on the International Space Station would commence). 'Space is a black curtain studded with stars,' he says. Against this dark background, the girders of a space station would glow luminously, with profound effects on depth perception. Far-away objects would appear close, but his experiments show that if an astronaut were to try and move closer, the tantalizing object would seem to shrink the nearer they got.

On alien planets, things could get eerier still. Our Lecturer recounts a trip to the desert in New Mexico, where he was staying on a mountain overlooking the wilderness. A mountain range beyond appeared to be a mere twenty miles away, when it was in fact triple that distance – impossibly far for anyone to walk carrying enough food and water for survival. 'After the misty English climate, the dry air of the desert gave a totally misleading indication of the distance of the mountains.' On alien planets with atmospheres very different to our own, we should expect the same dangerous illusions. Shadows, too, give us an important idea of depth. 'Heaven knows what happens to human perception on a world having two suns,' Gregory muses.

But if such alien worlds pose a danger, they also offer an exciting opportunity in Gregory's eyes. After all, these are not experiments we can carry out on Earth. 'It may well be that in discovering space we learn about ourselves … it is important to use the space travel situation to learn more about perception and its limitations, not only for the benefit of the astronaut, but so that we come to understand perception more fully.' And Gregory has another optimistic message. If perception is something we can learn, as his own research has shown, we might be able to adapt to seeing – and living – in these unfamiliar lands.

From the archive . . .

The public was divided by the choice of artwork selected for the front of the pamphlet, according to reports in the press. The image of an eye peering out from within an ear, was – according to an article in the *Medical News* on 1 December 1967 – 'described variously as "horrific" and "very clever".'

Gregory also wrote to RI director George Porter the month before, discussing the numerous demonstrations that would take place during the Lectures (see next page).

Lecture programme (front cover)

I enclose a recent paper of mine outlining a theory of the evolutionary origin of eyes and brains, and a possible very close connection between their development. I would quite like to make this the theme of probably the first lecture , to be illustrated with working models of primitive eyes. This would be great fun and so far as I know has never been done before. It would introduce them straight away to the idea that one can study perception as an "objective" problem, impinging on instrument design etc. When we get on to human perception and we look at illusions and other weird things which one sees directly, as "subjective" phenomena, they would get a feel for the double edge of these problems, without being sucked too far into the miasma of metaphysics.

The other paper I enclose (Eye Movements and the Stability of the visual world) illustrates how we can show them in a sense "subjective" phenomena, in this case after-images, and use them for discovering underlying mechanisms which should ultimately be traced out in the physical structure and function of the neural system. The importance here is that this kind of experiment can tell physiologists what to look for, and can give meaning and significance to recorded activity. I regard this as a very important point, sometimes neglected by physiologists who feel they can go it alone.

I aim at producing a fairly full synopsis by the end of next week. I do appreciate the importance of getting this planned as soon as possible, and will do my best.

Yours sincerely,

Richard L Gregory.

P.s. I saw Gerald Oster yesterday and he much enjoyed giving his Discourse.

FROM BRUCE HOOD …

Quite remarkably, two psychologists from Bristol University have given the Christmas Lectures, despite the fact that they traditionally tended to focus on the natural sciences. Hood was too young to watch Gregory's Lectures when they were first shown, and hasn't been able to see them since because there is no known recording of them, but Gregory would become a mentor to Hood, and Hood's department walls are decorated with photos from the series.

Richard had boundless enthusiasm. In 1999, I visited Bristol on sabbatical from Harvard and took up a chair in developmental psychology. When he came to my inaugural address, he was excited at the research I presented on children's naive understanding of the world around them.

We soon discovered that we had mutual interest in the big questions. What is consciousness? Can we really know anything? What is truth? How do children learn? I started dropping by his office and soon we would meet every Thursday at three for tea where he would regale me with his memoirs and anecdotes.

Richard taught me of the importance of communicating science. Not just to students but to everyone. He was not frivolous as some science communication can be, but rather a genuinely curious individual who never belittled any question or person he disagreed with. I regret that he died the year before I was selected to give the RI Christmas Lectures. I am not religious at all, but Richard Gregory was in my thoughts (and still is) throughout this fantastic time in my life. It was the joy of discovery and understanding that motivated Richard. I only hope that some of that rubbed off on me. 99

CHAPTER 5

SIGNALS FROM THE INTERIOR

Heinz Wolff
1975

✦

Our inner thoughts are not as private as we might think. Before the advent of brain scanners, Wolff takes us on a tour of some of the cutting-edge technologies used by doctors to understand their patients' bodies and minds without cutting them open. In this humorous Lecture series, we get to eavesdrop on the nervous system in action and read the mind of a teenage girl. Wolff also reveals the tell-tale signs we all give off about our personalities and emotions, and how people constantly use these to make decisions about others.

✦

Our bodies are alive with electricity, millions of small signals that can offer clues to what is happening in our heads. And electricity seems a particularly fitting place to start these Lectures, given that it is exactly 150 years since Michael Faraday, the so-called godfather of electricity, set up the Christmas Lectures in 1825 (although even he might have struggled to predict back then the idea that electricity could be harnessed to give us insights into the workings of the mind).

Wolff walks into the Lecture Theatre with wires protruding from his sleeves, and as he wrings his hands together a strange noise fills the room – 'like thunder rumbling in the background,' he says. What we are hearing is a cackle of electrical activity in his muscles as signals travelling from the brain instruct them to tense and contract, picked up by electrodes stuck to the back of his hand. This is a technique called electromyography – the first of many ways to listen to signals from the brain that Wolff will show us. 'It so happens that over the last fifty years or so technology has allowed us to find ways to amplify very small voltages indeed, signals that are only a few millionths of a volt in size,' he says. By comparison, a torch battery is one and a half volts and the voltage of a mains supply 240. 'So we're really dealing with very small electrical signals indeed.'

Wolff explains that these signals are in fact so small that if they are to travel from the brain to the muscles without fizzling out they need to be amplified along the way, like electrical cables laid across the Atlantic – a process that

Lecture programme (front cover)

slows them down dramatically. This might even explain a long-standing scientific puzzle, he muses. 'It has been said that the dinosaurs, of which there has been such a lot in the press recently, died out because their nerves were so long and it took such a long time for a message that somebody was nibbling their tails to reach their heads that they simply weren't quick enough on the uptake.' (It would be another five years before Luis Alvarez would propose the now widely accepted theory that the dinosaurs were wiped out by an asteroid.)

To demonstrate electromyography in more detail, Wolff is joined by Jason from the audience. 'I'm now going to ask Jason to have a little fight with me,' he says, 'and I hope that Jason is going to be gentle with me in deference to my age and falling hair.' Jason's bicep is wired up with electrodes, and as he tussles with Wolff in an arm wrestle we once again hear the thunderous sound of muscles in action. The harder he fights, the louder the noise, which makes this a useful tool for doctors to test whether a patient's muscles are working properly.

By placing electrodes on the head rather than our muscles we can listen directly to electrical activity in the brain (a technique known as electroencephalography), but the problem is that it's very hard to make sense of the signal, Wolff explains. The brain contains billions of nerve cells and is a hive of electrical and chemical activity. Trying to pick out any useful information from all that noise would be like flying over London in a helicopter that had been fitted with a giant microphone, he says. You would hear 'all the lavatories being filled and all the bars being let out and all the calls in the houses and all the radio sets that had been left on and all the discos going on all over the place'. Now imagine you wanted to pick out a conversation between Mr Smith and his wife: 'You wouldn't have a hope of doing so.'

Wolff describes how scientists can solve the problem using a technique called averaging, which amplifies the sound of specific brain signals so we can hear them over all the noise. It's as if your helicopter was now flying over Wembley stadium and suddenly a goal is scored and the 90,000-strong crowd cheers in unison. 'It is just possible if you were listening carefully enough from your helicopter that you might be able to detect that something abnormal was going on.' (At the time of Wolff's Lectures, electrodes on the scalp were the best bet for listening to the brain's activity from the outside, but we now have many more ways to see what's happening inside the brain, as we discover in subsequent Lectures.)

Another signal that can tell us much about what is going on in someone's head is their gaze, and Wolff is keen to showcase a new technology that is of great interest to advertisers as well as ergonomists, who work on equipment design.

By tracking in real time where someone is looking, we can reveal what sorts of things they are genuinely interested in without having to ask them. Small electrical signals are at play here too, Wolff explains, because the eye is like a battery – it is polarized from front to back. Carefully placed electrodes can record small changes in electrical activity that result from the eyes moving, and track the eyes.

Heinz Wolff (1928–2017)

Berlin-born Wolff moved to Britain with his family the day the Second World War started. He earned a degree in Physiology and Physics at University College London. Wolff is credited with coining the term 'bioengineering' – the application of engineering principles to biological problems. As well as his scientific contribution – he spent thirty years working for the Medical Research Council, before founding the Brunel Institute for Engineering and becoming an emeritus professor at Brunel University, London – Wolff is well known for drawing curious minds to the world of science and engineering through his numerous television broadcasts.

One willing volunteer, Mandy, has been wired up with electrodes stuck above and below her eye and on the front and back of her head, and as she moves her eyes according to Wolff's instructions, a small green dot darts about on a large screen. 'I'm now going to show Mandy the first picture,' says Wolff, as a grid of four images flashes up. We see an aeroplane, a picture of Margaret Thatcher, and some banknotes, but none of these piques her interest. It's the fourth image that instantly catches Mandy's eye as the green dot darts straight to a photo of a male model wearing nothing but trunks. 'Now see what she's interested in?' Wolff asks, to the sound of titters from the audience.

'Now just compose yourself again, Mandy,' Wolff says as the next set of pictures appears on screen. Mandy's eye is instantly caught by a picture of a young man with long hair and the crowd explodes with laughter again. 'I don't even know who it is; I'm not of this generation,' Wolff says as the young crowd shouts out: 'It's David Essex.' 'Is he a popstar?' Wolff continues, none the wiser.

Not all signals that come from the brain are obvious in their origins; many clues to our emotional states look the same as regular physical

Wolff reads Mandy's mind using an eye-tracking device

activity, Wolff explains. 'We must all be aware that our heart can go pitter-pat when we are excited, frightened or joyous; when somebody embarrasses us we blush because the blood vessels in our skin dilate without any need to increase our heat loss; that we can shiver with fright ... there are a whole host of physiological signals that result from emotional stimuli and not from the physiological need of the moment. And really,' he teases, picking up a bucket and chucking the contents at the front row of the audience, 'I feel

I want to do an experiment with you to illustrate one of those kinds.'

What looks like a sheet of water flies out, but everyone laughs as it turns out to be nothing more than polystyrene. Even so, a slow-motion playback of the action shows how the front row ducked and dived out of the way. These are involuntary reflexes, Wolff says. 'You had a number of reactions that you couldn't really help yourself showing to us.'

Only an extreme minority can avoid reacting in stressful situations like these, says Wolff – a group known as non-responders. 'I understand that some of the American astronauts were really chosen for their ability for somebody to sneak up behind them and fire a shot and they wouldn't even turn around to find out what happened.' (Wolff had a special interest in what happens to the body in space, and was made an honorary member of the European Space Agency in the same year he gave his Christmas Lectures.)

Hoping to show how these kinds of involuntary responses to stress can provide a window onto the mind, Wolff attempts a risky demonstration. 'We have a very gallant volunteer called Susan who is going to join me now for an experiment that almost certainly won't work,' he says. 'I'm going to subject Susan to some rather stiff interrogation in a moment, and we've joined her up to a device rather like a lie detector.'

As most of us can attest, the heart beats faster when we lie, so Susan has been wired up to an electrocardiograph that records her heart rate. Our skin can also give the game away, Wolff explains. It's a good insulator, so its electrical resistance is usually pretty high. When we sweat, however, tiny pores called sweat glands fill up with the salty fluid, and electricity passes through more easily. 'So the skin's resistance responses are linked to psychological states of mind.'

Susan picks a card from a deck and shows it to the audience before facing a barrage of questions about it, to which she must always answer 'no', and she remains remarkably cool under pressure. 'I think Susan probably would make a jolly good resistor to interrogation,' our Lecturer says, 'so I will recommend her to the European Space Programme.' There is just one instance where Susan's heart rate seems to have slowed, suggesting she held her breath during a question and was therefore shown to be lying.

Signals like these can give away our emotional state from one instant to the next, but other clues about our character are more permanent and it is these that Wolff tries to expose next. 'I've always been particularly interested in faces and the sort of messages we send out through our faces all the time.'

Wolff's fascination is with our apparently instinctive ability to recognize facial expressions. What are the ingredients that make one face seem surprised and another puzzled, for instance? 'We recognize a pattern without in any sense being aware of what the parts of the jigsaw actually are,' he says.

Facial expressions are just one form of non-verbal communication, but we also pick up similar signals from tone of voice, gestures and more. Ever the keen inventor, Wolff suspects that being able to work out how we do this could be very useful in medicine. 'I've spent the best part of my professional career either designing or improving or working with measuring instruments of various sorts of complexity used in medicine,' he says. And yet a large part of medical expertise seems to come down to hunch or intuition. 'What it means is a lot of the information doesn't come from the measuring instruments, but somehow or other is picked up by tentacles that the experienced person deploys to search the information atmosphere that surrounds this patient.' If only you knew what sort of signals they were picking up, you might be able to bottle this intuition by inventing instruments that look for them. 'In thinking about this I became interested in people who might know more about how to break the code. Who might those people be?' Wolff asks.

One group is cartoonists. With great economy of line, these artists manage to distil the characteristics and emotions of a person, and with just a few simple tweaks can alter and manipulate their expressions. 'So, they are one lot of people who must have to some extent broken the code, because they can presumably produce this to order.'

But there's another unlikely group of individuals who seem to have mastered non-verbal communication with very little effort. By now it would have been impossible for anyone watching the Lectures not to have spotted that the arms of many of the children in the theatre, and indeed entire rows of seats, hold teddy bears of various shapes and size, and we now discover why. 'I'm not a cartoonist so I wasn't able to do this research myself. But I am extremely partial to teddy bears,' Wolff admits. 'Now let me show you a slide or two.'

Wolff with an audience of teddy bears

Just as with cartoons, teddy bears somehow exude expression and personality and yet have very simple features. Wolff delights the audience with a slide show of teddy-bear portraits, subjecting each to a satirical character analysis. One serious-looking bear appears to be 'a master butcher in a small provincial town' according to our Lecturer. Another seems a bit naive. 'He hasn't been around a great deal. I wouldn't give much for his IQ.'

Wolff now turns his scrutiny to the bears in the audience. 'I think he likes his gin,' he says of one. 'I can just imagine him going along to the local and with one foot up on the bar holding forth on his experiences in India to all the other admiring bears.'

Wolff's interest in stuffed toys might be unusual, but he wasn't the first scientist intrigued by our ability to decipher meaning in faces. 'When I myself was still at school, perhaps about seventeen, I came across a book written by Sir Francis Galton … He was a nephew of Darwin and was an extremely versatile scientist,' he says.

Galton wondered whether there were common traits in the faces of people who had something in common. To find out, he took pictures of groups of people – for instance, those suffering from tuberculosis (or consumption, as it was known at the time) – and printed them so that each image was only partially exposed. It's as if each face were drawn on tracing paper; he could then stack them up and see whether any common features shone through. In fact, a hundred years before Wolff, Galton himself had stood in the same spot to give a discourse about these 'composite pictures'.

Wolff is clearly excited that the Christmas Lectures have given him the opportunity to try this idea out for himself. Six boys and six girls from the audience had come in the day before to be

Wolff creates a composite of six girls from the audience

photographed, and Wolff uses his lamp projector to superimpose their portraits one on top of the other to create a composite, just as Galton had done. The result is the average Royal Institution Christmas Lecture boy and girl. We can't deduce much from these composite mugshots, but 'perhaps in some years to come we can do this again to see how the average has changed,' Wolff says. 'I think this is rather good fun and maybe we've started a craze for getting one family photograph for the price of four.'

It is fun indeed, but Wolff hopes that composite images like these might tell us something useful about that intangible ability to read the faces of others. For instance, they could tell us what makes us want to vote for one politician over another. He compares two more examples made by his lab – one of Labour politicians from this year and another of Conservatives from the 1950s. Side by side 'there really is quite an appreciative difference,' he says. 'Now what the difference means, I wouldn't like to hazard a guess on. But they are again an average, a composite of faces, which in some way or other must distil something which appeals, for instance, to the voter at the moment and which might have appealed to the voter in the 1950s.'

As Wolff nears the end of his Lectures, he has another serious point to make. 'What is all this in aid of?' he asks. 'This is a Lecture with a light-hearted flavour to it. But this happens to be a hobbyhorse of mine at the moment, because I cannot help feeling that if we do understand non-verbal communication or the kind of signal flags which we fly all the time more thoroughly, we might learn to get on with one another better.'

From the archive ...

Ahead of the Lectures, Wolff put together some possible titles for the series:

```
BBC TELEVISION
_____

Proposed titlès for a series of 6 lectures suitable for the
Christmas programme of the Royal Institution.

An overall title of the series is "Inside Information"

1.   The message your heart sounds out.  ECG, haart sounds,
     possibly foetal heart detection by ultra-sound.

2.   How fast is your blood flowing?  Electromagnetic flow
     measurement, doppler ultra-sound, plethysmography.

3.   Analysing your breath, oxygen and carbon dioxide analysis,
     gas mixing in lung, breath alcohol.  Introduction to
     physical methods of gas analysis including gas-chromatography.

4.   What is your child-power?  Energy expenditure measurement,
     calorimetry, relation of heart rate and energy expenditure.

5.   Looking inside you without ex-rays.  Ultra-sound imaging
     techniques, fibre optics.

6.   Your gut calling.  Radio pills and other telemetry devices.
```

Concerned about whether he should include large pieces of equipment for his demonstrations, Wolff also wrote to TV producer Karl Sabbagh to ask for advice. The Lecturer also asked whether he should credit the various inventors and lenders of the numerous pieces of equipment he planned to use during his series (he did in fact give a long thank-you speech at the end of his last Lecture).

CLINICAL RESEARCH CENTRE
Bioengineering Division
Watford Road, Harrow, Middlesex HA1 3UJ

Medical Research Council
in association with
Northwick Park Hospital
Management Committee

18th July, 1975

K. Sabbagh, Esq.,
Room 6008,
B.B.C.,
Kensington House,
Richmond Way,
London, W.14.

Dear Karl,

I am not really sure whether this letter should go to you or
Sir George Porter.

I am now getting down to planning the details of the six
Christmas lectures and I require guidance on a number of points.

i) It is inevitable that I shall have to use gadgets and
equipment which:

a) have been invented by somebody other than myself and
will be borrowed from the inventor,

and/or

b) was actually being provided by courtesy of some third
party.

Is it customary to include some mention of this in the credits
associated with the programme to the effect that thanks are due
to Mr. A for the loan of one piece of apparatus and firm B for
another? Alternatively if individuals are concerned does one make
reference to them during the lecture along the lines

..... this flowmeter designed by my colleague
Dr. Wright .....?

RI director George Porter later wrote back to
Wolff, and was accommodating to say the least.
Whatever he needed, Porter assured, the Lecture
assistant Bill Coates would be able to make happen.
'As far as installing it in the theatre is concerned,
if you would like a couple of large elephants, Bill
Coates will get them in somehow!' he wrote.

CHAPTER 6

COMMON SENSE

Sir Colin Blakemore
1982

✧

Our senses are a window on the world, but can we trust them? In these Lectures, we embark on a magical journey into our own perceptual universe. Along the way, we discover how philosophers and scientists came to deal with the unsettling discovery that the world out there is often very different from that which we experience in our minds. The journey ends by asking how the brain manages to take all the information from our senses and turn them into the rich and meaningful experiences of feeling, seeing, touching, tasting and hearing that we all consciously experience inside our heads.

✧

Our story begins over five hundred years ago. 'Towards the end of the fifteenth century, Leonardo da Vinci turned his great mind to perhaps the biggest problem in science – the question of how the mind works,' says Blakemore. At the time, it was widely believed that it worked in three stages. First, the senses gathered information. The second stage involved intelligence, and the third was the formation of memories. Each stage was thought to take place in a series of successive cavities in the brain. The first one, as it was connected to the eye and analysed the senses, was known as the 'common sense'.

Lecture programme (front cover)

'Well, Leonardo was something of a revolutionary – he didn't like simply accepting authority,' Blakemore explains. Intent on carrying out his own experiments, da Vinci dissected an ox brain, filled the cavities with wax and then peeled the brain tissue away.

of nerves. Blakemore suggests that as multicellular organisms grew in size and complexity, their sense organs would have been too far from the muscles and other parts of the body to communicate with them directly. Something else was needed, 'and that something is, of course, the nervous system'.

To prove that the information from our senses is sent to the brain and processed there, Blakemore calls on his daughter Sophie to help him with a simple demonstration. He screens off one of her eyes, so it is hidden by a piece of card, and the television camera zooms in close on the other. Behind the screen, Blakemore flashes a light into his daughter's eye, and each time he does this, the audience can see how the other pupil shrinks and then expands again. The fact that both eyes were responding to light shining into just one of them proves that the reaction is coordinated by the brain and not the eye itself.

While on the subject of vision, his area of expertise, Blakemore describes how our sense organs are exquisitely sensitive. 'You've all had the experience of walking into a dark room and at first you can't see anything, but gradually as time goes on you begin to see more and more, and see very faint things that you couldn't have imagined that you would have seen when you first entered the room.' The retina in the eye is lined with thousands of rods and cones, receptors that detect light waves and turn them into electrical impulses for the brain to recreate into images of what we see (as Hartridge described in his 1926 Lectures; see page 23). The reason we are able to see so well even in the dark is because the rods – which we use to see in dim light – are so sensitive that they can detect just one quantum, the smallest physical package of light. 'So there the limit seems to be one of physics, not of biology.'

Despite the incredible acuity of our sense organs, however, all these sensory signals need to be sent to the brain and that's where biology lets us down, explains Blakemore. 'You see, however good biology has been at designing instruments of detection it hasn't done terribly well on designing cables.' Rather than being able to alter the voltage of a signal, as is the case with electrical cables, 'nerves transmit pulses and the pulses are always the same size'. Instead, to send a stronger signal, a stream of impulses is sent along a nerve fibre, making the whole system rather slow. 'This property of nerve fibres is the thing that restricts, ultimately, the performance of our sense organs.'

Sir Colin Blakemore (b. 1944)

Born in Stratford-upon-Avon, Blakemore studied medical sciences at Cambridge University and did a PhD in Optics at the University of California, Berkeley. He has worked in the medical schools of Cambridge and Oxford and was most recently Professor of Neuroscience and Philosophy at the School of Advanced Study, University of London, before becoming Yeung Kin Man Professor of Neuroscience at City University of Hong Kong in 2019. Blakemore's work has focused on vision and brain development, in particular brain plasticity – how brain cells reorganize themselves in response to the environment. He has held many prestigious positions including Chief Executive of the UK Medical Research Council, and is a member of twelve scientific academies, including the Royal Society and the Chinese Academy of Engineering.

Next, Blakemore goes on to show how signals from our various senses are combined by the brain, and he is very excited to introduce his next guest, Michael Broadbent, who is renowned for his fantastic sense of taste as 'one of the best-known wine masters in this country'. When given a red wine to blind-taste, he manages to describe it with astonishing accuracy, getting the year and the grape right, and even getting close to pinpointing the location of the chateau. The next red wine bamboozles Michael, however, until the trick is revealed. It is in fact a white wine that has been coloured. 'We did this deliberately, I should say, because we wanted to try and show the importance of colour in determining the total judgement of taste,' Blakemore confesses. (We now understand much more about how the brain combines information from many senses at once to give us our sensory experiences. Listening to high-pitched music can make food taste sharper, certain colours are associated with sweetness, and people rate the same food as tasting better and denser when eaten from a heavier bowl, to give just a few examples.)

As well as the senses that we are all aware of, Blakemore introduces one less-celebrated sense – the ability to know where we are in relation to gravity and where each body part is in relation to others. This is known as proprioception. To give us an example, our Lecturer turns to a demonstration we have seen before (Hill did the same thing in 1926, but used a video rather than a live animal; see page 18), welcoming in a ginger cat named George. 'Cats, as you all know, are very good at landing on their feet. I hope I'm going to demonstrate that by holding George upside down,' Blakemore says. 'Watch him very carefully.' He counts down and the audience members hold their breath as he drops the cat onto a foam mattress. Of course, George lands the right way up, and Blakemore repeats the experiment, this time with the lights out, the whole thing filmed on an infrared camera. The footage is played back in slow motion and we can see how the cat rotates as he falls to the ground, landing on his feet once more. Because he can do it in total darkness, George must be using information from his balance organs.

Our understanding of our position in space is largely down to three tiny fluid-filled canals in the inner ear that form what is known as the vestibular apparatus. As we move around, so does the fluid, pushing and bending tiny hair cells that send signals to the brain, updating it about our position and keeping us balanced and on our feet, much like George the cat.

The whole system can get overwhelmed when we spin around fast and stop suddenly. It's such a familiar experience that the audience probably doesn't need it demonstrated, but still they giggle as Blakemore whizzes his eldest daughter, Sarah Jane, around on a spinning chair and she staggers off into his arms, unable to walk in a straight line.

There is a clever way to avoid this problem, however, as Blakemore's next guest demonstrates. A ballet dancer, dressed in a tutu, pirouettes dramatically into the room. Why didn't she fall over, Blakemore asks, after all that spinning? Slow-motion footage of her entrance reveals the secret. With each turn, the dancer keeps her head perfectly still and facing forwards, turning only her body. Then at the last moment she whips her head round. We feel dizzy after spinning because the fluid in the ear keeps moving for a while. This technique, which is called spotting, 'helps to avoid this problem of disturbance produced by steady rotation of the balance organs in the ear,' Blakemore explains. (As well as the fact that spotting minimizes head movement when spinning, later studies have also shown that ballet dancers' brains adapt to all the spinning, making them feel less dizzy.)

A ballet dancer demonstrates how to avoid getting dizzy

Even with such intelligent sense organs, the information we get from them would be useless without the brain to make sense of it all, and how it pulls off this feat is the subject of Blakemore's final Lecture. 'The brain may have started in evolution as a very simple form of connection between sense organs and muscles … but it's become so much more than that – a magical instrument that goes beyond the senses.'

New technologies can help us to understand how the brain interprets the senses, and Blakemore shows a picture of a 'very modern' method – a positron-emission tomography scanner. It allows neurologists to see which areas of the brain become active when various senses are stimulated, so we can now create maps on the surface of the brain to represent where the senses are processed.

These maps will vary from animal to animal. Humans have lots of nerve endings in our fingertips and lips, so the brain is bombarded by signals from these areas and therefore a much larger area of the brain is dedicated to processing them than less sensitive body parts like our upper arms.

It's a different story for Blakemore's next guest, who can be heard squealing in the wings before making its appearance in the arms of the Lecturer's assistant. It's a baby pig from London Zoo, and the audience gets a close-up of its snout, which is constantly twitching. The pig uses it to explore the ground much like we use our fingers to discover the world, and it is packed with nerve fibres.

In fact, studies of the pig's brain found 'a quite remarkable sort of map,' Blakemore says. Aside from the snout, 'the rest of the body had virtually no representation at all in the pig's brain,' he says. 'So, each animal then has a map of its sensory

*A pig's snout is densely packed with nerve fibres,
like our fingertips*

world, and a map which is distorted according to
the importance of each bit.'

How does this pattern of activity actually create
the feeling of perception? That is down to the nerve
cells themselves in these brain areas, our Lecturer
suggests. 'The very cells which make up the map,
those cells are interpreting the signals that they
receive. They are the elements of perception.'

'So the nerve cells can behave intelligently,' says
Blakemore. But the brain is also more than the

hole somewhere out there to the side [of the eye]?' he asks. 'It's about as big as your fist at arm's length but you never see it at all.' This blind spot is caused by an area of the retina called the optic disc, where all the nerves and blood vessels come in, and there are no light receptors. 'Your brain somehow fills in that missing gap in the information because it has the expectation that there really are no holes in the world.' (Hartridge also revealed this blind spot to his audience in his 1946 Lectures; see page 29).

This is just one of many in-built expectations about the world around us that the brain relies on to create a seamless experience despite problems with the information coming in. These expectations combine with our senses, and thanks to them, 'we need only a little information from the sense organs to produce the right perceptions,' says Blakemore.

Another example has to do with timing. By the time messages from our senses reach the brain, they are already out of date. 'We live in a world which is actually behind the real world,' Blakemore points out. As a result, the brain has to work as a prediction machine, accounting for the delay and getting ahead of it. A young volunteer, Lorenzo, demonstrates this when he is asked to follow a pendulum with his finger. When the Lecturer moves the ball himself in an unpredictable manner, it is impossible for Lorenzo to keep up. But when the pendulum is allowed to swing in a predictable manner, Lorenzo can track it accurately with his finger, as his brain can easily predict where the ball will go next. 'Lorenzo's brain, within a fraction of a second, calculated that predictable motion and he was therefore able to subtract out the delay in his own brain.'

One of Blakemore's research interests is whether these expectations about the world are learned, or built in to the brain from birth. Even babies can track objects with their eyes, so some of these expectations must be innate, he says. But humans, like other animals, can also learn to build new expectations. To demonstrate, a box is brought to the desk and the audience is clearly thrilled to discover it contains six tiny chicks. 'Here we have some baby chicks which hatched in the Royal Institution just a couple of days ago. Their problem is that they haven't got a mother,' says Blakemore, appealing to his audience for anyone who might be able to provide one.

On cue, Blakemore's youngest daughter Jessica walks down to the desk holding a toy duck. The audience has a good laugh when the Lecturer

Blakemore demonstrates imprinting with the help of newly-hatched chicks

realizes there are no batteries in the toy (it turned out that one of his other daughters had removed the batteries in an attempt to sabotage her sister's big moment), but he goes ahead and moves the duck himself over the desk, and the chicks follow eagerly. These chicks were reared with the toy in their box, he explains. 'They've become imprinted on it as if it's their artificial mother.'

'So the sensory systems of animals depend on their expectations of the world,' says Blakemore as he brings his Lectures to a close. 'Some of those expectations are built into the animals when they're born, some of them are learned. And man, perhaps the supremely intelligent animal, can continue learning very quickly about his senses all through his life.'

 FROM COLIN BLAKEMORE . . .

My most vivid experience in the run-up to the Lectures was when I was visiting Switzerland for the summer to work at the University of Lausanne. It was already September and I really had done very little to prepare for the Lectures.

For some reason the telephone at our apartment wasn't working. I went outside to find out why, and found that a technician was working on the overhead cables. And as I was talking to him he was monitoring the line, and he said: 'Oh my goodness, there is a call coming in for you.' So I climbed up and took a call from George Porter (who was Director of the Royal Institution at the time) from the top of the telephone pole in Lausanne.

He was incredibly gentle and discreet but was obviously, below the surface, having a little panic about whether I'd done anything to prepare for the Lectures. And I remember thinking, 'What am I going to do to stall?' He asked me if there was any way they could help, for instance with the preparation of the demonstrations. So I thought, 'OK, this is a great opportunity; I'll just throw a few wild ideas out that are so improbable it will take weeks for them to sort it out and that will give me a chance to work on the Lectures.'

So I said: 'Yes, George, I'd like an electric eel, a ballet dancer, and a sniffer dog.' I'd expected him to put the phone down and call me back in a couple of weeks. But he said to just hang on a sec. And he came back about ten minutes later and said, 'Well, we've got all of those. Is there anything else you need?'

That was a bit terrifying. So I confessed and I said: 'Well actually, George, it would help a lot if I'd written or prepared anything. But I am going to do it.' So it was all a bit of a panic, but that's the way I work.

From the archive . . .

Blakemore wrote to the TV producer for the Lectures, a few months before they were due to commence, to outline the specific content and focus of his six lectures, with an emphasis on the way the brain 'almost magically' creates perceptions that are 'much richer than the sensory data on which they are based', as well as the ways in which our sensory analysis is restricted.

So, one major emphasis in the lectures will be on the restricted nature of sensory analysis, but on the other hand, I should have to emphasise the way in which this very limited information is used almost magically by the brain to create perceptions which are in a way much richer than the sensory data on which they are based. That richness must, of course, be provided in part by central analysis in the brain which is influenced by memory of past experiences, by genetically constrained mechanisms and by previous learning and developmental modification. The discussion of this theme will give me lots of opportunity to show nice demonstrations of perceptual phenomena of course.

Finally, I don't want to fall into the trap (as I said before) of dealing with each sense organ alone and in turn. I want to discuss the relationships between the senses and the way that they collaborate with each other despite enormous physical and logical difficulty in such collaboration providing an integrated view of the world. I should, for instance, discuss the relationship between vision and touch (that raises all sorts of interesting philosophical questions which I think should not be impossible to explain to school-children). Another nice example is provided by the integration of auditory and visual information to build up a single picture of the spatial relationships between objects in the world. I should talk about experiments on adaptation to disturbances of the relationship between different senses. For instance, it is very easy to demonstrate rapid adaptation to the wearing of a prism which displaces the visual field by a few degrees.

I hope that you will agree that although some of the particular discussion must obviously overlap that in certain of The Brain programmes, never-theless the general organization of the Christmas Lectures that I propose is really rather different. I feel sure that with adequate consultation between us, we can arrive at a format that will minimise the duplication of material and yet will be entertaining. I hope that you agree.

Yours ever

Colin

Colin Blakemore

CHAPTER 7

JOURNEY TO THE CENTRES OF THE BRAIN

Baroness Susan Greenfield

1994

✧

This Lecture series is full of firsts. Not only is it the first time in the 170 year-long history of the Christmas Lectures that they are to be given by a woman; it is also the first time they focus entirely on the brain. Greenfield takes us on a fascinating quest to try and understand how this lump of tissue makes us who we are. To get there, she lays bare the mechanics of the brain before asking some important questions – which don't always have easy answers.

✧

'We're about to go on a journey,' begins Greenfield, surrounded by jars of pickled brains and model heads. But this is no ordinary journey: 'It's a journey that you could take inside this very room and yet it's a far harder journey, far far harder, than for example going to the moon, because it's a journey into our own brains. To find out how our brains work.'

The first stop on the journey is North America in the mid-nineteenth century, where a young man was working on a railway gang. As Phineas Gage pushed dynamite down into a hole with a large tamping iron, the explosive ignited prematurely, sending the rod right up through his skull. 'Now, you might imagine that this would blow Phineas to pieces, but that wasn't the case,' says Greenfield, holding a huge metal rod up to her temple to make her point. Astoundingly, when he came round, Gage seemed pretty

Lecture programme
(front cover)

similar to before, 'even though he had a bar sticking out of his head'.

As time went on, however, it became clear that something had changed – his personality. Previously quiet and well-mannered, Gage was now reckless. He swore a lot. As Greenfield puts it, he became a 'bad-tempered, thoroughly unpleasant individual'. Picking up a real human brain preserved in liquid, Greenfield reveals the significance of this freak accident, which has become an iconic story in the history of neuroscience. It proved 'that your very personality, your individuality, is at the mercy of this simple lump of tissue'.

This is the issue at the heart of the Greenfield's Lectures; how our brains make us who we are. 'They're the very essence of you,' she says. 'In these Lectures we're going to try and find out how that individuality, that specialness, came about.'

To do that, Greenfield first considers how the brain works, and we hear about some of the structures within it. Distinct regions look quite different, like the crumpled surface of the brain (the cortex) and the cauliflower-like cerebellum at the back, which suggests that each one has a very different function.

Zooming in, the audience sees an electron micrograph image of the brain that reveals dark round blobs amid what looks like a tangle of wires. These are the brain's most basic components, cells called neurons, and their multitude of connections. 'It looks like a real jungle,' Greenfield muses.

Taking this analogy further to demonstrate the staggering complexity of the brain, Greenfield compares it to the Amazon, the vastest forest in the world. The Amazon contains 100 billion trees, and this is the same number as the number of neurons in your brain (although, incidentally, since these Lectures were given, the estimated number of trees in the Amazon has shot up). Each of these neurons will send between ten and a hundred thousand connections to other neurons. If you were to try to count all the connections in the cortex alone, Greenfield adds, it would take you a whopping 32 million years (at a rate of one per second).

Not all animals have such complex brains, and before turning in more detail to how these cells communicate, Greenfield demonstrates just how exquisitely adapted our brains are to the environment, with the help of some live zoo animals. Both our Lecturer and the audience seem enraptured by the

Greenfield holds up a snake brain next to a live python

first of these, a large python. Greenfield strokes it enthusiastically while explaining that its brain is small and smooth, with an extra-large area dedicated to smell.

Her next guest is an owl called Max. His brain is larger than a snake's, but still not as large as that belonging to the next creature to come out. The audience gasps as an exotic-looking mandrill walks onto the stage, with a striking blue face and red nose. This primate is a much closer relative to humans, and is much more interested and aware of its surroundings, than the previous guests, Greenfield points out, as she tentatively hands it a banana. Its brain reflects this, she says, picking up a chimpanzee brain (a close enough approximation to that of a mandrill), which has a deeply folded surface. These folds in the brain's outer layer, the cortex, are vital to primate intelligence because they give the brain a much larger surface area, meaning it can be packed full of billions of neurons.

How these neurons do their job is the subject of the next Lecture. Greenfield begins by questioning two common metaphors for the brain. With its electrical wiring and ordered modules, it is often

Max is introduced to the audience

compared to a computer. But it could also be thought of as a seething, bubbling cauldron full of chemicals, working a mysterious kind of magic. Which of these analogies truly reflects the nature of the brain is a problem that has puzzled neuroscientists for over a century, she admits.

Like the computer, the brain relies on electricity, and to demonstrate this important principle a giant model of a brain cell is brought into the theatre. We can see that the cell has branches, called dendrites (after the Greek word for 'tree'), through which it receives electrical messages from neighbouring cells. At rest, the cell contains charged atoms of potassium, Greenfield explains, while on the outside there are charged sodium atoms. If enough neighbouring cells send signals to the dendrites of this cell, 'something very special happens'. The sodium rushes into the cell, and the potassium rushes out, causing a change in voltage strong enough to create an electrical signal. This travels down the main body of the cell, sending the message on to its neighbour.

But the model reveals a new problem. There is a gap, called a synapse, between each brain cell. 'It's like driving down to the sea before the days of the

Channel Tunnel,' says Greenfield. 'Unless you have a car that can swim on water, you're stuck.'

The next guest offers a clue to how the signal crosses this gap. On comes Russell, who works at the British Museum, carrying a quiver of arrows used by Amazonian hunters. 'This clue is very, very, very, very hazardous,' warns Greenfield, who isn't allowed to handle the arrows herself. 'Even though it's thirty years old, it's still so toxic that no one but Russell can touch it, and we had to lock it up in a safe overnight while here at the Royal Institution.'

These poisonous arrows are fired through an eight-foot blow gun, and can instantly paralyse their unfortunate victims – firm proof that chemicals, not just electricity, can interfere with the nervous system. And we now know that this is exactly how nerve cells communicate, Greenfield explains. When electrical signals reach the synapse, they trigger the release of specific chemicals that cross the gap and pass the message on to the next cell, 'a bit like getting into a boat when you come to the river'.

So, the brain is both a computer and a cauldron and, while that might seem overly complicated, it offers a big advantage. Electrical signals are all alike, but by using chemicals we can vary the type of message that is passed from one cell to another. This is fundamental to the bigger question of how the brain makes us who we are. By varying the amounts and types of chemicals the brain uses to communicate, you automatically have a system of variation built in, says Greenfield. 'A system of variation which can then be used for adaption, for flexibility, for learning, for memory. For being one person rather than another.' This is key to building our individuality. 'We have the precision of the computer, we have the diversity and richness of a cauldron of chemicals, and with that combination we can become unique people.'

But the chemistry of the brain isn't the only thing that builds our unique characters. Like our personalities, the brain develops as we get older. We spend much longer as dependent babies than any other animal, and for good reason. At birth, the human brain is the same size as that of a chimpanzee, measuring 350 cubic centimetres, but it continues to grow at a mind-boggling rate – as much as a quarter of a million neurons per minute, says Greenfield. In order for our brains to be fully formed at birth, pregnancy would last twenty-one months, she adds, and our heads would be so big we would never make it out of the birth canal.

A year after birth, our neurons have started to make firm connections and are covered in insulation, which helps them to orchestrate complex movements. To demonstrate this dexterity, Greenfield is joined by one-year-old Sebastian, who delights the audience with his ability to pick up Smarties (and promptly make them disappear in his mouth!).

Picking up a human brain that has been plasticized, Greenfield ponders another facet of individuality that seems to emerge as we enter childhood: the differences between male and female brains. Sex is set as early as nine weeks in the womb, but you would struggle to tell just by looking at the brain in

Greenfield is joined by one-year-old Sebastian

her hand the sex of its owner. (There are a couple of differences; for instance, men tend to be bigger than women, so their brains are often bigger too.)

But girls and boys often have different attitudes, says Greenfield. She plays a video of young children answering questions about which toys they like, and the sorts of jobs they want when they grow up. True to stereotype, the boys shun the idea of playing with dolls, and aspire to become train drivers, while the girls favour domestic roles. 'Where those attitudes come from, of course, is currently a source of great debate.' (The debate continues to this day, although the role of culture is seen as increasingly important, with biological differences on a spectrum that can apply to both genders.)

By the time we approach adulthood, the brain has changed in dramatic and surprising ways. Rather than making new connections, 'at sixteen you've been losing connections since the age of two,' Greenfield reveals. You might think that's bad news – after all, at this point you will have lost half of the connections in your brain, she adds. But this is actually a crucial process that sculpts the brain in response to our experiences. After a flurry of connections are made during early childhood, the brain prunes away the connections and circuits we don't use, while strengthening those we use the most. This is key to developing skills such as learning languages (and is why new accents are harder to pick up after childhood) or sports, as each of us is then left with the most useful and important combinations of circuits to suit our lives.

'Something as simple as a change in what you're doing can actually change the connections in your brain,' says Greenfield. To demonstrate this idea in the real world, two large glass cages are wheeled on, each one home to a rat. One rodent has nothing but sawdust in the cage, whereas the other has an exciting playground of toys and mirrors. Greenfield explains that simply living in this varied environment has changed this rat's brain: it has more than twice the number of connections as its neighbour, who has nothing to play with. Could it be that by pruning unused connections and sculpting the brain in this way, experiences are what shape our individual personalities?

This quest to find where the seat of our individuality lies, says Greenfield, is 'one of the hardest questions of brain research'. Just by looking at a brain, we would know nothing of the person that it came from, 'whether he or she liked listening to music or walking in the country, whether they were kind, whether they had a sense of humour …'

One hint at the answer to this puzzle comes from two people who have more in common than just their brains, and Greenfield welcomes identical twins Dominic and Joshua on stage. Despite their shared genetics and upbringing, when our Lecturer quizzes them about their earliest memories, they give her very different answers. 'Could it be that if we pursued memory, if we explored memory, this might be a road in to looking at individuality?' Greenfield asks. After all, memory takes our experiences and builds them into the brain.

There is one person who perhaps has done more than anyone else to help demystify how memories affect our identity, and Greenfield relays the legend of a man referred to by scientists at that time only as HM (this was standard practice for scientific case studies, to protect privacy. After the man's death in 2008, his full name, Henry Molaison, was made public).

Molaison suffered from severe seizures, and in the mid-1950s, at the age of twenty-seven, he underwent experimental brain surgery to try to tackle the problem. During the radical operation, parts of both sides of his brain were removed, explains Greenfield, 'but it might surprise you to learn that this operation has never, ever, ever been performed subsequently, and the reason is because of the terrible consequences. When HM recovered from the surgery it turned out that he had no memory.'

Baroness Susan Greenfield (b. 1950)

Born in London, the daughter of an electrician and a dancer, Greenfield was the first of her immediate family to go to university. She studied psychology at Oxford before going on to do a PhD in neurochemistry. Since then she has held research fellowships at Oxford, the College de France Paris, and NYU Medical Center New York. Her research interests include diseases of the brain, as well as consciousness, and our relationship with technology. She was Director of the Royal Institution from 1998 to 2010. Greenfield became a life peer in 2001 and received a CBE for her work on the public understanding of science in 2010.

While he could remember things that had happened before the operation, Molaison could not form new memories. Nothing was going into storage. It was as if everything he did, every day, he did for the first time. 'Imagine what it's like to be really trapped in the present,' Greenfield says.

This bizarre existence turned Molaison into the subject of countless research studies, and he became possibly the most important patient in brain research. One question we could now begin to answer was where memories are stored in the brain. 'It's easy to think of memory like some attic at the top of your house, where you've stored a lot of files that can then be retrieved,' says Greenfield. But we know that the brain is a vast tangle of cells and networks. In that jungle of brain cells, where is the memory warehouse?

Molaison's surgery destroyed the hippocampi – two seahorse-shaped lobes, one on either side of the brain, suggesting these could be involved (and we now have plenty of other evidence that these are involved in memory, in particular moving memories from short- to long-term storage, and in spatial memory, which helps with navigation).

But other areas must be involved too, because

studies of alcoholics – who also suffer from memory impairment – show that they have damage to other parts of the brain. Instead of there being one warehouse, concludes Greenfield, it seems that laying down memories is a process that calls on contributions from many areas of the brain.

A slightly gory experiment sheds more light on the problem. Brain surgery can be performed on people while they are awake (the brain has no pain receptors, so this doesn't actually hurt), and Greenfield describes how, in the 1950s, a surgeon named Wilder Penfield decided to make the most of the fact that patients' brains were exposed during surgery. Penfield electrically stimulated the surface of brains of hundreds of patients to see if anything changed about their state of consciousness. 'In quite a few cases something very interesting occurred,' says Greenfield. When he ran the current through a part of the brain called the temporal cortex, 'suddenly in the middle of the operating theatre they had a very vivid memory'.

The brain didn't seem to be behaving like a warehouse, however, because the memories were inconsistent. Sometimes the same area was stimulated but gave rise to very different memories.

Sometimes the same memory cropped up after Penfield stimulated a totally different part of the cortex. It's as if you went up to the attic to retrieve a document and found a different one in the same place each time, or found the same document in several places at once, Greenfield says. One explanation is that memories are actually stored as circuits of brain cells, rather than as individual neurons. That way you might activate different neurons that are part of the same circuit and trigger the same memory, as in Penfield's experiments.

Turning her attention from where memories are made to exactly how they are stored, Greenfield recounts a classic experiment involving two identical kittens, where one of them is taught to raise a paw. Sadly, we don't get to meet any live kittens, but the audience sees a graph of what happens to the connections between synapses in the two cats. In one brain area involved in raising the paw, the kitten that was trained ended up with many more of these connections between brain cells. Greenfield explains how, when one neuron repeatedly fires, signalling to a neighbouring neuron, the repeated release of chemicals in the gap between them changes the structure of the cell almost permanently.

Just as our experiences shape the brain by pruning away the connections we don't often use, they also strengthen the ones we do use. 'So, it seems then that even at this very basic level of the synapse we can say that this is important, this is the building block, somehow, of memory.'

Before the Lectures draw to a close, we are treated to a rendition by a band called the Neurons. As well as providing a musical interlude, they illustrate an important point that we've come to appreciate about the brain: it is more than the sum of its parts. 'Coming to the end of this particular journey we can think about different brain regions like instruments playing as the Neurons did – as a wonderful, cohesive whole.'

From the archive . . .

Peter Day, then Director of the RI, wrote to St James's Palace, inviting Prince Charles and the young princes to attend Greenfield's Lectures. He mentions the fact that Queen Victoria's sons, Prince Albert Edward and Prince Alfred, attended Faraday's Lectures on 'The Distinctive Properties of the Common Metals' in 1855. The palace replied to say that unfortunately the princes were unable to attend that year, but requested information for the following year's Lectures.

PROFESSOR PETER DAY FRS
Director and Resident Professor of Chemistry

Cdr RJ Aylard RN
Private Secretary to His Royal
Highness The Prince of Wales
St James's Palace
London SW1A 1BS

11 August 1994

The Royal Institution Christmas Lectures

I am sure you know that the Royal Institution's Christmas Lectures, now entering their 165th season, are entertaining events designed to bring science alive to a young audience through demonstrations and skilful illustration. Each year they are given in our Lecture Theatre in Albemarle Street in front of about 450 young people in the days just before and after Christmas, when they are also recorded for broadcasting on BBC2 television. This year the dates in question are Saturday 17 December, Tuesday 20 December, Thursday 22 December, Thursday 29 December and Saturday 31 December, at 3.00 pm.

This year, for the very first time since Michael Faraday gave the first lectures in 1826, the lecturer will be a woman, Dr Susan Greenfield, a pharmacologist from Oxford University. She will be talking about how the brain works. It occurred to me that Princes William and Harry are now of an age at which they might find this event entertaining, so I am writing to ask if they would like to come on one of the afternoons. Of course, it would be marvellous if the Prince of Wales were able to accompany them. There is a famous precedent in that the Prince Consort brought the two young Princes Albert Edward and Alfred to Michael Faraday's Christmas Lectures in 1855-56. I enclose a picture depicting this occasion. More recently, in 1976, His Royal Highness The Duke of Kent brought his son, The Earl of St Andrews, and the two Princes Andrew and Edward.

Please let me know whether my idea finds favour. I shall be delighted to send you more information should you need it.

Greenfield was thrilled to have given the Christmas Lectures, and wrote to Day to thank the RI for a 'marvellous experience' that had changed her life.

— *UNIVERSITY OF OXFORD* —

UNIVERSITY DEPARTMENT OF PHARMACOLOGY

Mansfield Road · Oxford · OX1 3QT

Dr S A Greenfield M.A., D.Phil
University Lecturer
Fellow & Tutor Lincoln College

23 January 1995

Professor Peter Day
The Royal Institution of Great Britain
21 Albemarle Street
London
W1X 4BS

Dear Peter

Thank you for your letter of 4th January 1995. I also feel I have to express my gratitude to you for letting me have this marvellous opportunity, it is an experience that I can honestly say has really changed my life; I found the whole exercise exciting, enjoyable and instructive. It was amazing to feel part of such a strong team effort and I am particularly indebted, of course, to William without whom the whole series would not have been half the success it was.

Thank you again for giving me such a marvellous experience and I look forward to seeing you on 20th and discussing Japan, Singapore, etc.

Very best wishes.

Yours sincerely

[signature]

Susan Greenfield

CHAPTER 8

RISE OF THE ROBOTS

Kevin Warwick

2000

✧

It is the start of the new millennium, and Warwick asks us to consider a not-so-distant time in the future when robots could have intelligence to rival our own. Introducing a veritable robot zoo along the way, his humorous Lectures reveal how machines are being equipped with many facets of human cognition, including sensory perception and emotions. We also discover how technology might enhance our own brains, and the audience is treated to a true glimpse of the future, as Warwick predicts with uncanny accuracy many of the big issues around artificial intelligence that trouble us today.

✧

The auditorium is dramatically lit with purple searchlights and the desk covered in various machines, including a pair of large robotic arms. 'Robots raise some very controversial questions,' says Warwick, addressing his young audience for the first time. 'What do we want them to do? What decisions do we want them to take? And what impact will they have on society?'

To begin to answer these questions we need to know what robots are capable of, and Warwick first considers androids – robots that look and behave a bit like humans. In order to move and communicate, androids need intelligent senses such as ours, and Warwick is excited to introduce one such robot. 'He's travelled more than seven thousand miles from Japan to be with us today,' he says, revealing a state-of-the-art Japanese robot that has been flown over especially for the Lectures. The sad-looking robot has human features, with big eyes, a nose, eyebrows, mouth and large metallic ears. Like humans, its predominant sense is vision and we see how, using cameras for eyes, it can follow a light about (cameras work much like the retina at the back of the eye). Those large ears also contain microphones for hearing, and the robot startles when someone shouts behind it.

Warwick introduces a Japanese robot with human-like senses

But robots can also be endowed with senses that go beyond human capabilities, and next we meet the Seven Dwarf robots, which come from Warwick's own university, Reading. These busy little machines scurry about the floor of the Lecture Theatre and, as Warwick takes refuge up on the lecture desk, he describes how they use ultrasound to find their way around. When the ultrasound signal hits an object it bounces back, alerting the robot that there's something in its path.

As we have learned in several Lectures, our brains have evolved to be finely tuned to vision, the sense we tend to rely on most. But attempts to develop robots with superhuman senses like ultrasound could also enhance our own sensory capabilities, especially when something goes wrong.

'What would it be like to have not the senses you or I have, but the senses of this robot?' Warwick asks. One keen volunteer, Joe, gets the chance to find out, with the help of an ultrasonic headset that sends out the same sorts of signals as the Dwarf robots. Warwick calls on several members of the audience to act as a dense 'virtual forest', and a blindfolded Joe has to pick his way through the human trees without bumping into any of them. Each time Joe gets near to someone, he hears an electronic piano-like noise in the headset, and using these sounds as a guide, he manages to squeeze his way through the tightly packed throng without touching anyone. So these sorts of superhuman senses aren't reserved for robotics research, Warwick points out. A headset like this one could be useful for someone who is blind to navigate the environment.

If humans are going to interact successfully with robots, there's another important facet of human nature that we need to consider, and that is our emotions, says Warwick. To demonstrate, he's been running an experiment over the course of a weekend with two young audience members. Down from

*Joe uses ultrasound to find his way through a
'forest' of volunteers*

their seats come brother and sister Rowan and Russ,
accompanied by an adorable robot dog called Aibo.
'What we did was to ask Russ and Rowan if they
would give up their own dog that they have, and swap
it for Aibo for a weekend. And this is what happened.'

Over at Russ and Rowan's house, a film has
been made as the experiment unfolded, and we see
footage of the siblings saying goodbye to their dog,
before getting to know Aibo, playing with him and
training him. Back in the Lecture Theatre, Warwick
asks them whether they would permanently keep
the robot in exchange for their own living, breathing
canine. Astonishingly, both say they would. 'Okay,

so I'll come later and pick up your dog and you can keep Aibo,' he teases.

What makes Aibo so irresistible is that it engages with our emotions much like a real dog, and that's not surprising when we consider – as Sophie Scott shows in her 2017 Lectures (see page 176) – that our emotions are a universal means of communication, with deep evolutionary roots. When we struggle to understand emotions, we find it hard to understand others at all.

We also know, as Wolff showed us in Chapter 5 (see page 79), that signals from the brain in response to our emotional states cause all sorts of physiological changes in our bodies, from a racing heart to sweaty palms, which give away what we think and feel.

So if robots are ever going to be able to interact intelligently with humans, they need to begin to understand our emotions. With this in mind, we are shown a video of Kismet, a highly advanced robot in America that has the ability to respond to the tone and emotion in human voices. Kismet smiles when it receives praise, which raises a laugh from the audience. 'But Kismet is not particularly intelligent, it's … something of a little illusion in many ways,' Warwick explains (in fact emotion recognition remains a tricky subject in robots, as we discover later in Sophie Scott's Lectures).

In his penultimate Lecture, Warwick turns to a question that is close to his heart: what if we were able to merge humans and machines? 'Can we look to a future where we're not just humans alone but we become half biological, half mechanical?' he asks. 'Are we going to have a world in the future where we're cyborgs?' A cyborg is something that is part human, part machine, but enhances human capabilities, Warwick explains.

Futuristic as that sounds, it's already happening. Prosthetic limbs can be controlled by the electrical

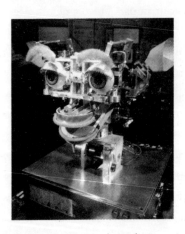

Kismet can recognize and simulate emotions

signals that the brain sends out to our muscles telling them how to move. To demonstrate, Warwick is joined by colleagues from his own department, equipped with a prosthetic arm that uses electromyography, the signals given off by muscles, to carry out the exact movements a person intends their hand to make.

But Warwick considers cyborgs to be more extreme still. 'My idea of a cyborg is a human who is permanently connected with technology. Perhaps the human and technology become one.' If we could connect the brain directly to technology, we might end up with the power to control it using our minds, he says, and technology would also have the power to control us. 'The human brain is amazingly complex but already there have been developments to link the brain directly to the outside world.'

Our next guest, Benjamin Glover, is a young boy who has had a cochlear implant to help him to hear. The role of the cochlea in the ear is to convert sound waves into electrical signals to be sent to the brain. It does so with the help of thousands of hair cells, tiny receptors that move in response to vibrations created by sound waves in the ear. When these cells move, they turn the vibrations into electrical signals that are sent via the auditory nerve to the brain. If these cells are damaged, as in Benjamin's case, it can have a profound effect on hearing, so an implant is fitted to the skull and artificially mimics the role of the hair cells, directly turning sound waves into a message the brain can process.

The next cyborg we hear about is already familiar to the audience. 'A couple of years ago, I had an implant just like this surgically put into my arm,' Warwick reveals, showing us a small computer chip stuck onto his arm. With the implant in place, he was able to open doors in his university without touching them, turn the lights on automatically, and switch on his computer when he went near it. It's as if he had his keys and computer passwords all built into his body.

Warwick describes the next stages of his experiment (which is called Project Cyborg). We hear how he would like to have electrodes implanted into a nerve in his arm that could intercept electrical signals from his brain that relate to the senses or movement. The implant could then send the information to a computer, so it would effectively be decoding and storing some of the contents of the human brain. If the signals were sent back to the nervous system, they might trigger the sensations of pain or cause movement, he says. It might even be possible to

Kevin Warwick (b. 1954)

Coventry-born Warwick left school at the age of sixteen to join British Telecom as an apprentice, before going on to do a degree at Aston University and then a PhD at Imperial College London. At the time of the Lectures, he was Professor of Cybernetics at the University of Reading, and he is now Deputy Vice-Chancellor of Research at Coventry University. As well as his work on robotics and artificial intelligence, Warwick captured the public imagination with Project Cyborg, a series of experiments carried out on his own body, which he discusses in the Lectures. The work earned him the monikers 'The world's first cyborg' and 'Captain Cyborg'.

connect up two people in this way; Warwick ultimately wants his wife to be given a similar implant, so that they could share sensations directly from one body to another, and Warwick muses over what it might be like to experience someone else's pain signals. 'Will you know what it feels like? Will you feel the same pain? The thing is, we

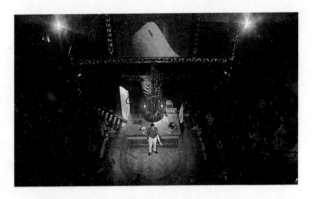

*Warwick shows the audience the chip that was
implanted into his arm*

don't know yet – that's what science is all about.'
(Warwick later went on to successfully carry out
both of these next steps of his experiment. When
his implant was connected to his wife's, every time
she closed her hand a pulse was sent to his brain.
He describes this as a new form of very intimate
communication. 'It was a form of telegraphy,' he
says now.) Of course, this sort of technology would
have mind-boggling applications. Being able to
send signals from one person's nervous system to
another's would pave the way for communicating
by thoughts alone.

In his final Lecture, Warwick turns his attention

from cyborgs back to robots, and considers whether they could ever truly be intelligent. 'Can we give them minds of their own?' he asks, before reading an extract from Arthur C. Clarke's novel *2001: A Space Odyssey*, in which a computer named Hal can no longer be controlled by humans and eventually takes control of their spaceship. At the time of the Lectures, it is very nearly the year 2001, and Warwick asks just how far this vision is from reality.

Perhaps the most famous test of robot intelligence was devised by computer scientist Alan Turing in 1950. A computer passes the Turing test if it can fool us into believing it is in fact a human from the way it answers questions, Warwick explains. In other words, a human can't tell whether the answers are coming from another human or from a machine, and at the time of the Lectures no computer had ever passed this test.

Recreating the Turing test in the Lecture Theatre, two computers have been set up outside the room. One will be controlled by a volunteer, Warwick explains, and the other by a computer program. Children from the audience will be probing the computers by sending them a series of questions, and it's the job of the audience and viewers at home to decide, based on the answers, which are coming from the young girl and which from a machine. As this final Lecture is being broadcast live on television, a phone number and email address flash up on the screen inviting viewers at home to send in their own questions, too.

TEXTED & E-MAILED THEMES FOR TURING TEST

ARE YOU CAPABLE OF LYING?

WHAT IS A TELETUBBIE?

WHAT MAKES YOU SAD?

WHAT'S YOUR FAVOURITE SUBJECT AT SCHOOL?

TEXTED & E-MAILED THEMES FOR TURING TEST

IF YOU HAD THE CHOICE, WOULD YOU HAVE BLUE OR GREEN EYES?

WHAT THINGS INTEREST YOU?

HAVE YOU HAD A HEADACHE?

WHAT IS YOUR MOTHER'S NAME?

Questions for the Turing test sent in by viewers

In the meantime, exploring the question of machine intelligence further, we meet thirteen-year-old

British junior chess champion Gawain Jones, who is in the middle of a game of chess against a computer program called Fritz. 'Mathematicians have estimated that on the chess board there are more positions possible than there are atoms in the universe, so it's quite a complex game,' Warwick points out.

Just three years earlier, the then world chess champion Garry Kasparov was beaten by a chess-playing computer called Deep Blue. On the big screen we see a video of an interview Kasparov gave just after losing to the machine, in which he is clearly spooked by the experience. 'When I see something that is well beyond my understanding I'm scared, and that was something well beyond my understanding. I have no idea what's happening behind the curtain.'

But Warwick pulls back the curtain for his audience, explaining the trick computers use to achieve this apparent feat of intelligence. The big advantage they have over human brains is speed, so they can run through thousands of possible moves much faster than the human mind ever could. This kind of intelligence is very limited, however. 'It must be better if we can give them something like common sense,' he says.

From the day we are born, humans learn and our brains develop as a result of experience (see Colin Blakemore's Lectures, page 97, for more on this). As the Swiss psychologist Jean Piaget said, intelligence is what you use when you don't know what to do, and that's based on past experiences and being faced with new situations. For computers to do the same, we'd need to take them into all sorts of situations and program them to deal with each one in turn, which would be extremely laborious, Warwick explains. But what if, like humans, we could 'start them off rather like babies and give them the capability to learn'.

Known as machine learning, this is a very exciting topic in robotics, and to delve into it in more detail, Warwick welcomes on a little robot called Nibbler, who starts zipping around the Lecture Theatre floor. 'It's been given a goal in life and that is to move forwards and not bump into things,' he says. On cue, Nibbler repeatedly bumps into the desk, much to the delight of the audience. But that's a good thing, Warwick explains, as Nibbler is learning from the experience using an artificial neural network, a kind of artificial brain that allows it to learn by trial and error. So, this robot is learning a bit like babies do – partly through programming and partly through experience.

As Warwick talks, the robot continues to explore and gradually stops colliding with things. It has managed to do this with just forty-nine neurons, 'so it's got as much brain processing as a slug'. That's a long way off the 100 billion neurons of the human brain, but much larger neural networks are already in use, says Warwick, for instance in the Stock Exchange where vast amounts of data need to be processed very fast. 'At the present time people are being replaced by artificial neural networks in many stock exchanges simply because the machines are better. The artificial brain is better than the human.' (These demonstrations of machine learning were well ahead of their time, and this kind of artificial intelligence has since become a very topical issue.)

As we near the end of the Lectures, Warwick ponders whether robots might ever surpass human intelligence. This seems unlikely from the results of the Turing test demonstration at the start of the Lecture; the audience wasn't fooled, and most people correctly guessed which answers were being given by a machine and which were those of the young volunteer.

To find out why, we hear from David Hamill, the scientist who created the computer that was competing in the test. 'It's really just a box of tricks,' he says. 'It's not got any intelligence at all.' To demonstrate, Hamill asks our Lecturer to think up a question for the machine. 'Do you like football?' he asks. 'I saw *Titanic* on the TV the other day,' comes the response, and the audience giggles. 'I can see the relationship between Manchester United and *Titanic*,' Warwick quips back.

The problem is that the machine has simply been programmed to recognize certain words and construct answers based on them. 'It has no idea of what the world is about.' Turing might have been disappointed by the result, having predicted that by the year 2000 his test would have been passed by a computer (whether or not it has been passed to this day is controversial, but many – including Warwick – accept that a computer passed the test in 2014).

Whatever progress is made with machine learning, it's only of limited use if robots can't pass their knowledge on to future generations as humans do. The ability of humans to not only learn from their experiences but also teach those lessons to others is thought to be a crucial facet of humanity that allowed us to build our complex technological societies. And as anyone with children will know, much of how they learn is by observing what others do. 'That's how life progresses,' says Warwick.

Our Lecturer welcomes back Nibbler, who is now accompanied by another little robot called Zoidberg. As Nibbler explores the environment again, his companion stays quite still. 'That's because it doesn't know what to do,' Warwick explains. But when Nibbler feels it has learned enough, it will teach Zoidberg what to do using radio signals. The audience look enthralled as Nibbler sends a message to Zoidberg, who then begins to move about with ease. Without being programmed by a human at all, 'this robot is behaving as it has learned to behave from another robot teaching it,' Warwick says.

This ability of robots to learn, and even to evolve, on their own poses big problems for those working with and using the systems. Sounding a warning bell well ahead of his time, Warwick leaves the audience considering an issue that has become one of the most pressing technological problems of our age: if machines are programmed to work things out on their own, once they get going it can be hard to know how these algorithms are doing what they do. This is especially problematic if they are making decisions for us that are then impacting on society, as Warwick foresaw at the start of his Lectures; it has come to be known as the 'black-box problem' of machine learning. 'Realistically, as *Homo sapiens*, we can't really have any idea what's going on in the brain of a computer network,' says Warwick, 'and that could be very difficult if we're trying to control them.'

FROM KEVIN WARWICK . . .

Almost twenty years after giving his Lectures, Warwick still remembers how it felt to be asked to do them. 'It's something wonderful, but you instantly look at the list of people that have done it before. It scares the pants off you, to be honest.'

Much of the material covered in the Lectures seemed very prescient in hindsight, although some of Warwick's views were considered pretty radical at the time. Some of these were picked up by the press in the run-up to the broadcast, garnering negative headlines. 'Among the more controversial pronouncements made by Prof Warwick ... is the prediction that, before long, intelligent robots will take over the world', mocked one reporter from the *Sunday Telegraph*. But today, controversies over the use of artificial intelligence are rife. 'There are now people like Elon Musk, even Stephen Hawking before he died, pointing to the threats of artificial intelligence. If it gets too much, if we let it get out of hand, it could be very dangerous. That was something I was trying to point out back then. But some people didn't like me saying things like that,' he recalls. Many of the other technological advances that seemed very unlikely at the time of the Christmas Lectures have also become a reality. 'So, I think they were very futuristic in a lot of the things we were looking at, which have now come to fruition.'

From the archive . . .

RI director Susan Greenfield wrote to Warwick in April that year to invite him to give the Christmas Lectures following an impressive Lecture he'd given at the RI recently.

FROM PROFESSOR SUSAN GREENFIELD CBE
DIRECTOR
AND FULLERIAN PROFESSOR OF PHYSIOLOGY

Professor Kevin Warwick
Department of Cybernetics
The University of Reading
Whiteknights
PO Box 225
Reading   RG6 6AY

April 3, 2000

Dear Kevin

I am writing to you with what I hope will be an exciting proposal. Would you be willing to give the Royal Institution Christmas Lectures this year? Following your spectacular Public Lecture, I am convinced that you would have just the right subject and tone to make it a really fabulous series. Of course, there will be many things to discuss, but I hope that if you are still receptive to the idea, we might start to proceed with a discussion on the telephone. I would be very grateful if you would telephone my PA, Gayna Clark, on ▓▓▓▓▓▓▓▓, as soon as possible, so that we might set up a call to develop the idea further.

I look forward to hearing from you.

All very best wishes

Professor Susan Greenfield
*Dictated by Professor Greenfield
and signed in her absence*

CHAPTER 9

MEET YOUR BRAIN

Bruce Hood

2011

How would you feel if you discovered you are in fact blind for much of the day, your memories are made up and what you think you see isn't really there? In recent years, great advances have been made in our understanding of the brain and in this lively series of Lectures, Hood exposes some of the ways we have found the brain conjures up the unique experience of what it is to be human. Along the way he pulls the rug from under us by demonstrating with clever tricks and illusions how our world is not as it seems.

'Let me introduce myself. I am Bruce Hood and I am a scientist interested in the human brain,' our Lecturer begins from a set designed to look like a 1950s horror movie. 'Actually, when I say I am Bruce Hood, what I should have said is *this* is Bruce Hood,' he says, pointing to his head. 'Because everything I am is really a product of my brain … it's our brain who makes us who we are.'

Hinting at some of the surprising revelations to come, Hood introduces two young audience members – Charlie and Iona. 'As you can plainly see, Charlie is much taller than Iona. But sometimes, reality is not what it seems.'

First, however, he says he wants us to meet 'someone else here. Or rather, someone who is here no longer.' On a plinth in the centre of the stage a

An entry ticket for Hood's Lectures

spotlight illuminates a real human brain. Its donation to science was agreed by its owner before they died, says Hood as he picks it up, 'so that the rest of us could discover more about the workings of this most amazing organ – a thing that is so wondrous and yet so mysterious that we still do not fully understand how it works'.

As a developmental psychologist, Hood is interested in how the brain changes as we grow older, but he also has a fascination with the way it creates the illusion of our experience of the world, and why, because of the way the brain works, it can trick us into believing very unlikely things.

To explore this idea, Hood begins with the subject of his PhD: vision. 'Most people think vision is like a camera,' he says. But we know from studies that the brain only processes the central part of our field of vision, an area about the size of your thumb if you were to hold it out horizontally at arm's length. In theory then, the rest should be blurry, and yet we don't go about the world with most of our visual field a fuzzy mess. The reason, Hood reveals, is that our eyes are constantly moving, darting about four or five times every second. Without trying, we are continuously sampling our surroundings, and storing the information to build a complete and complex picture of the world around us.

This explanation creates another mystery, however. If our eyes are constantly on the move, we should see the world in flux, making everything seem distorted. 'It would make you seasick,' says Hood. So the brain does something dramatic to fix this. Each time we make one of these tiny eye movements (called saccades), it simply cuts out the information sent from the eyes while they move, so we don't experience this movement at all. It's as if we go blind for a fraction of a second. And the brain then edits out all these tiny gaps to recreate our seamless sense of vision.

There's an easy way to demonstrate this remarkable fact, and Hood asks for help from a volunteer, Amy. He tells her to peer down into a handheld mirror and to look back and forth, first at her left eye and then the right. As the cameraman zooms in on Amy's face, we see on a big screen how her eyes dart from side to side. But Amy herself says she can't see her own eyes moving in the mirror, and is shocked when the video footage is played back on the screen, clearly proving her wrong.

'We can't see our eyes moving at all,' explains Hood. 'No matter how hard you try, your brain is making you blind.' If you add up all that time, you would be blind for about two hours of the waking day. 'Clearly the mind is full of tricks that keeps the world looking rich and full of detail.'

Scattering some coffee beans onto a tray, Hood moves on to another trick of the mind. He asks the audience if they can see any images forming in the random arrangement of beans. 'A mouse,' shouts someone, and the Lecture Theatre fills with chatter as others call out their suggestions. The reason we find meaning in random patterns is that 'the brain is always trying to impose structure and order,' Hood explains. This is also the fundamental reason why some people believe in the supernatural. To prove it, Hood conjures a ghost in front of our eyes, with the help of the Kanizsa illusion, named after the Italian psychologist who first described it, Gaetano Kanizsa (we were first introduced to another example of this illusion by Richard Gregory, who was an important mentor to Hood, in Chapter 4).

On a board, he places four circles, each with a quarter cut out (imagine each one looking like Pac-Man). When the four shapes align with the missing tranches lined up, it suddenly looks as if there is a white square in the middle. The brain is filling in the missing information to make sense of it, says Hood. 'Your brain assumes that the only way each pie can have a piece missing is because there must be a white square on top of them.'

Although the square is a ghost, the brain thinks it's real, and if you were to test the visual area of the brain, the same neurons would be firing as when you see a real square. 'As far as the brain is concerned, the square is really there.'

Illusions, Hood says, reiterating a theme of several

Hood explains the Kanizsa illusion

other Lectures, are not just trivial games but can give us powerful insights into how the brain interprets the world and creates the experience of everyday life.

If the audience weren't already convinced, he calls back Charlie and Iona. We have already seen that Charlie is several feet taller than Iona, but that is about to change. A cameraman follows the pair out of the Lecture Theatre into another room, which has a tiled black-and-white floor and green walls. Standing in one corner, Charlie hunches and towers over Iona. But when they swap places, the audience gasps – as they both walk across the room Iona seems to grow while Charlie shrinks to a fraction of her height.

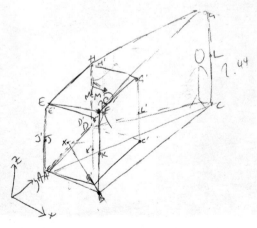

A working sketch of the Ames room demonstration

This is a famous optical illusion, an Ames room (after American scientist Adelbert Ames Jr, who invented it) – a fake room in which the floor is slanted and the walls are not parallel, with one corner of the room bigger and further away than the other. When filmed from a certain angle, the room looks to be a normal box-shape. And even though we know people can't grow and shrink in front of our eyes, the brain has an expectation from past experience that rooms tend to have flat floors and parallel walls, explains Hood, so it assumes this must be the case here, and instead comes to the

Hood reveals how the Ames room works

conclusion that one person is unfeasibly big and the other impossibly small. Your brain is creating the experience of what you see.

Having shown that what we perceive is often fabricated by the brain, in his second Lecture, Hood tackles a very controversial illusion; the illusion that we are in charge of our own minds. Our brains are constantly being bombarded by all sorts of information from our senses, and if we were made aware of all of it, we'd never get anything done (just think how many faces you see in a day as you walk around a town, and yet you don't consciously notice most of them unless something stands out – your brain must be selecting which ones are worth your attention). So from these reams of information, how does the brain decide what to focus on, and what information to keep?

Key to answering this question is memory, and losing long-term memories, for instance when the brain is damaged, can be devastating. 'You lose your identity, because who we are is really the sum of our memories,' says Hood.

Yet in spite of their importance, our memories too can be deceptive. We often think of them like a photograph of the past, stored somewhere in the filing cabinet of the brain. But to demonstrate an important point about memories – that they aren't fixed in this way but are much more fluid – Hood gives the audience a simple memory test.

Reading out a list of words, he asks us to remember as many as we can. Many of the words seem related, for instance 'thread', 'pin', 'sharp', 'prick' and 'haystack'. 'Now let's test your memory,' says Hood. 'Hands up if I said the word "needle".' The vast majority of the people in the audience raise their hand, even though it wasn't on the list at all. 'I implanted a memory,' Hood smiles. Words are stored in the brain in networks, and the word needle was triggered by all the other words, which stimulated the association to it.

Rather than being like a photograph, every time you remember something, you reconstruct it from other experiences stored in your brain (an idea that fellow Lecturer Bartlett put forward well ahead of his time; see page 41). This leads us to a tantalizing question. 'If your memories can be wrong, and memories are the key to your identity: well, who are you?'

This is a question that has troubled philosophers for a long time, but 'the answer must lie with the brain because people can be changed when the brain gets damaged,' Hood says, recounting the unfortunate story of Phineas Gage whose personality changed dramatically after a metal rod shot through his head (which we also heard about in detail from Susan Greenfield; see page 116).

Gage suffered damage to his frontal lobes, which are widely connected to other regions of the brain and control all sorts of aspects of behaviour, judgement, decision making, coordination and memory. They are like the 'chief executives in our "Head Office",' says Hood.

You don't need a metal rod through the head to change the way the frontal lobes work. A much simpler way is to succumb to the effects of alcohol, which are well known to interfere with judgement and coordination, as well as affecting our personalities. This is also the last brain area to mature as we grow up, which is why young people can be very impulsive. During teenage years, Hood explains, we see one of the most dramatic rewirings of the frontal lobes, which is why it can be such a tumultuous time.

Returning to the question of whether we are in control of our own minds at all, Hood points out that as well as controlling our memories and our personalities, our brain also takes charge of what we pay attention to in the first place. Because we evolved to be highly attentive to food and predators, it's almost as if we shine a spotlight on areas of interest at the expense of other things.

In a daring experiment to carry out live, the stage of the Lecture Theatre is filled with an entire troupe of jugglers, who set about a complicated routine. Hood instructs the audience to count how many times the red juggling clubs change hands, and after

Hood on the Lecture Theatre stage with one of his many props

the performance he quizzes the crowd about whether they noticed anything unusual.

Remarkably, it's only when we are played back some slow-motion footage of the juggling act that most of the audience notice for the first time someone dressed as a gorilla walking across the stage among the jugglers. 'It's a pretty good demonstration that you don't notice everything [that's going on around you],' Hood says, to laughter and applause.

So the brain is regulating behaviour, including what we pay attention to, how we learn, what we remember, says Hood, often without us realizing. Which goes to show there's 'not one "me" that's in control'.

The subject of Hood's third and final Lecture is also one of his research interests, the social brain, and he begins with the promise of another impressive trick. 'You don't need to be psychic to read someone's mind,' he says. We do it all the time, every time we try and put ourselves in someone else's shoes. 'In fact,' he tells his audience, 'you are the best mind reader in the animal kingdom.'

We become brilliant mind readers during childhood, Hood explains. It's the research and development stage of life, when we are absorbing information from the world around us and learning to become human. Even before babies are born, they can learn to recognize their mother's voice, and in one study, pregnant women read aloud Dr Seuss stories; once their babies were born, they preferred their mother's telling of the stories to anyone else's, Hood says.

Young babies also show a strong preference for human faces over other patterns. Hood holds up three dots in the shape of a face in front of eleven-month-old baby Finn, who follows it intently with his gaze.

There is even an area of the brain dedicated to processing faces, and anything that resembles a face can trigger it, says Hood, as he delights the audience with pictures of toast, taps and other objects that look like faces pulling all sorts of expressions. 'We are programmed to find faces anywhere,' he says. Strikingly, when this area of the brain is damaged, people can fail to recognize familiar faces, even their own friends and family. Faces are so important to the social brain because they teach us about emotions, which are strong social signals essential for our survival.

Bruce Hood

Born in Canada (we don't know exactly when, as he doesn't share his birth-date publicly), Hood studied psychology at the University of Dundee and then received his PhD from Cambridge University. He worked in the US before returning to the UK to Bristol University where he became Professor of Developmental Psychology. Inspired by mentor and previous Christmas Lecturer Richard Gregory, Hood has become a prolific science communicator and enjoys using performance to communicate his work. He has written several popular science books, including *Supersense*, about the natural origins of supernatural beliefs. He is the founder of Speakezee, the world's largest academic speakers platform. After the Lectures were broadcast in the UK, he also took them to Japan and Singapore.

Emotions also bring us together as a social group, and Hood says that to demonstrate this idea, he will need to provide a blood sample for an experiment. Making a show of how much he dislikes needles, he allows a woman in a white lab coat to apply a tourniquet to his arm, before she pulls out an enormous needle to giggles and gasps from the audience. 'There's just going to be a sharp scratch,' she says, but before it goes any further, Hood jumps off the couch.

The entire performance, it turns out, was a ruse, and the real experiment was taking place in the audience. 'A lot of you didn't look very happy when you saw that needle, and we have one person in the audience who's been wearing a heart rate monitor,' Hood reveals. On the big screen, we are shown how the volunteer's heart rate shot up dramatically just as he thought the needle was going in to our Lecturer's arm. 'You empathize physically and emotionally with someone when you watch them suffering,' says Hood. This is why moments of extreme emotion, for instance fear, can be almost unbearable to watch.

It's only recently that we discovered a set of neurons in the brain that seem to copy the emotional state of others, called the mirror neuron system. These fire at the same time as we see something happening to someone else, as if it were happening to us; as if our brains are synchronizing. These neurons could also be behind our amazing ability to learn by imitating, says Hood, which forms such an important part of early life.

There's another ingredient needed if you want to be a great mind reader. Before you can put yourself in someone else's shoes, you need to have a sense of self-awareness yourself. Young babies and many animals can't recognize themselves in a mirror, which is used by scientists as a good test of whether they have a sense of self. We meet one such animal – a Siamese fighter fish called Simon. When a mirror is placed behind his tank, he violently attacks the apparent interloper again and again. 'Because he doesn't have a sense of self, he doesn't recognize that it's his own reflection,' explains Hood.

In sharp contrast, we are shown video footage of an elephant called Happy, who lives in the Bronx Zoo in New York. She has some tape stuck to her head, and when she spots it in her reflection she tries to remove it, showing that she does have a sense of self-recognition. Young children, too, fail this mirror test, and it's only once we grow up and develop a sense of who we are that we can then begin to understand that others have a different point of view, Hood explains.

As well as making us incredible mind readers, there's another reason why this social brain is so important. As the Lectures draw to a close for another year, a world population clock on the big screen shows that there are over 7 billion humans on Earth, and the number grows as Hood talks. 'In the last hour or so, the world's population has already risen by another ten thousand brains,' he says. 'We are all going to have to get along if we are going to survive as a species. It's a challenge, but we have specially evolved brains for getting on with others. And really that's one of the main joys of life.'

 FROM BRUCE HOOD . . .

Hood's Lectures were so popular that they became the first to ever be rerun on television, something Hood generously attributes to his subject matter. 'Everyone is a psychologist to some extent and I think people are intrinsically interested in the mind, what makes people different.'

That's not to say things always went smoothly, especially with the live animals. One of the most unpredictable was the Siamese fighting fish. 'We had to acclimatize it to the Royal Institution, so it came in a week beforehand and was sitting in the production room at the back, and we kept wondering whether or not anything was going to happen because the fish wasn't performing. So, we didn't know whether it would attack its own image,' Hood recalls. When the demonstration did work, Hood heard a cheer go up in the production room through his earpiece. Then there was the moment when someone had to walk through the set dressed as a gorilla and hope the audience wouldn't notice. '[Psychologist] Dan Simons who did the original demonstration told me, "That's never going to work live, you cannot get that to work live." And I said, "Well, we're going to have a crack at it," and blow me, it bloody well worked. It was really quite remarkable. It was the finale demonstration – there was so much riding on it.'

CHAPTER 10

THE LANGUAGE OF LIFE

Sophie Scott

2017

✧

Our ability to speak is one of the things that defines humanity, but it may not be as special as we like to think. Scott reveals how speech might have evolved as an accidental afterthought, and shows us that there are many other important ways to communicate, often without making a sound. We also look to the future, asking whether we will ever be able to communicate with other species, have meaningful conversations with machines, and even be able to speak to other beings in outer space.

✧

Cackling laughter ricochets through the auditorium as Scott begins her first Lecture. It's not the audience laughing (although with comedian Scott as their guide, plenty of laughs will be had over the course of the series), but a recording very similar to one that is now travelling through the universe. Holding a golden phonograph record, Scott describes how a similar disc called *The Sounds of Earth* has been sent into space attached to the NASA *Voyager* spacecraft, the most distant manmade object from Earth. One of the sounds selected to be on it is laughter, so this could be the first human sounds aliens ever hear, she says.

Of all the messages we could be sending to extraterrestrials, laughter might seem a strange choice. But 'laughter is one of mankind's most important sound communications,' says Scott. To demonstrate how powerful it is, the audience is shown a video of one of her favourite research participants, a man called Doug Collins, who is often told he has the most contagious laugh in the world. He sounds a bit like a donkey braying, which sets off the audience in fits of giggles.

Other animals laugh too, and Scott welcomes her first guest onto the stage, a brown-and-white rat called Mould. To make a rat laugh, all you have to do is tickle it, and we discover that the best place to tickle a rat is where you tickle a person – the armpits. The rat makes a high-pitched chirping noise, and we know this is a kind of laughter, says Scott, because they emit the sound in the same situations as when humans laugh.

Sixty-five million years ago, we shared a common ancestor with rats, so it could be that laughter survived all this time because it's such an important communication sound for mammals. It might even be one of the very first sounds we made, Scott suggests.

But communication sounds are useless if we can't also hear and decode them. When a sound is created, for instance by someone clapping their

A ticket for Scott's Lectures

hands, molecules in the air create sound waves, which radiate out like a cloud.

Because the brain needs information in an electrical form, it's the job of the ear to turn these vibrations in the air into electrical signals that the brain can decode. 'The entire ear is a machine for turning the vibrations in the air into something your brain can hear as sound,' says Scott. First, the outside of the ear, the pinna, funnels the vibrating air molecules down to the real ear, tucked inside your head. A model of this inner ear reveals how the vibrating air molecules hit the eardrum and push against it, and how the movement created by the beating of this drum transmits the vibration to the three tiniest bones in the body. These miniscule bones relay the movement on to the cochlea, a fluid-filled tube that starts to move with the vibrations. Finally, tiny hair cells in the cochlea bob up and down, creating the electrical signal that is sent to the brain.

Humans are exceptionally good at rapidly modifying the sounds we make, which is a key ingredient for our ability to speak, and it's this that Scott explores next. To demonstrate just how versatile our vocal abilities are, we are joined by a special guest, one of the world's greatest beatboxers,

Reeps, who treats the young audience to an impressive performance. On a screen, we also see a video of what happened when Reeps was asked to beatbox while being monitored by an MRI machine, a type of medical scanner that can give detailed images of our insides. In the film, a cross-section of Reeps' head and neck reveals the extent to which his vocal tract changes while he beatboxes. The teenagers in the audience look particularly impressed as he manages to produce two different sounds at once. 'That's technically not supposed to be possible. Apparently no one told you,' Scott jokes.

Aside from beatboxers, there are other vocalists, such as opera singers, who can produce a magnificent range of sounds, and compared to these kinds of impressive vocal gymnastics human speech is pretty simple. We actually do the bare minimum when we talk to each other, Scott says, so it might be that we evolved remarkable vocal abilities before we ever applied them to speech. Our ancestors may have used their complex vocal skills to impress mates or defend their territories, and the incredible human ability to talk evolved later on by accident. 'Once we'd evolved this absolutely extraordinary musical

An opera singer and beatboxer Reeps show off their vocal skills

instrument of the human voice, maybe speech was almost an afterthought. An afterthought, of course, that has created the world we live in through the gift of language.'

Not all communication happens with sound, however, and one of the simplest ways to share information is using smells. Smells are made of chemical molecules, part of a body or object that has been sent into the air, Scott explains. 'Everything from bacteria to blue whales is made of chemicals, so the simplest way to send a message is just to leave some of those chemicals behind.'

To demonstrate the fact that many animals live in this world of smells, two brave volunteers join Scott on stage and allow snakes to slither over them, and we see how the creatures' tongues are continuously sampling and tasting the air around them. The smells animals use to communicate with each other are called pheromones, and like many other animals, snakes rely on an organ in the roof of their mouths called the vomeronasal organ. They dip their tongue into this organ to bring the pheromones they have sampled into contact with nerves there, sending signals straight to the brain.

Humans can't pick up pheromones like snakes do, and to demonstrate why that is Scott shows us three skulls from different primates – a lemur, an ancestor of apes, and a modern human. With each one, the face becomes much flatter, with smaller noses, which means there's much less space for smells to be detected. But there's another important reason. Even though our brains are bigger than those of other mammals and our early relatives, the smell areas are comparatively much smaller. 'Smell is downplayed right from the start in humans,' says Scott. On the other hand, the areas for processing vision and sound are much larger than in many other mammals, 'probably because vision and hearing have great advantages for human communication,' she says.

Sophie Scott (b. 1966)

Born in Blackburn, Lancashire, Scott studied life sciences at the Polytechnic of Central London (now called the University of Westminster) and then earned a PhD in cognitive neuroscience at University College London (UCL). After a stint at Cambridge University, Scott returned to UCL in 1998, where she has worked since.

In her role as Deputy Director and Head of the Speech Communications Group at UCL's Institute of Cognitive Neuroscience, Scott's research concerns the neuroscience of voices, speech and laughter. She is a member of the British Psychological Society, the Society for Neuroscience, the cognitive Neuroscience Society and the Experimental Psychology Society. She was elected a Fellow of the Academy of Medical Sciences in 2012 and a Fellow of the British Academy in 2016. Scott is also recognized for her public engagement work, including her stand-up comedy.

The big problem with using smells to communicate is that they can only move at the same rate as the air around them. To send more complex messages, you need a speedier system, and that's the advantage of being primed for vision.

Proving just how good humans are at picking up silent visual communication signals, Scott turns to one of her specialist areas of research: emotions. 'Our bodies give away a huge amount about our inner feelings but our faces can be even more expressive,' she says.

On a large screen we are shown a tedious video of a London skyline accompanied by elevator music, and Scott asks the audience to count how many birds they can spot in the film. As everyone concentrates on the movie, a ghoulish face jumps out in the middle of the shot, causing the audience to leap from their seats. 'I've got to tell you, that was a trick – there were no birds,' admits Scott. Instead, she wanted to prove just how similarly we all respond to a fearful situation.

Fear is just one of a number of emotions that seem to be universal across human populations. They are the same wherever you go, almost like a map of human emotions that we can all experience and recognize, says Scott, regardless of your culture or what languages you speak. 'The fact you find them across all human cultures is a hint they come from deeper in our evolutionary story.'

This was an idea popularized by Charles Darwin himself as early as 1872, in his book *The Expression of the Emotions in Man and Animals*. In it he suggested that perhaps emotions had the same function in humans and animals, which could be why they are evolutionarily important. Another reason for universal emotions might be that we need them to be totally unambiguous, Scott adds. 'If I am frightened, you should be frightened too.'

But even if some of them are universal, not everyone finds it easy to interpret emotions. People on the autism spectrum can have issues understanding what the emotions of others might mean and what their own emotions are conveying, Scott says.

Her next guest might be able to help. Scott introduces Zeno, a humanoid robot that is being used to help children on the autism spectrum to learn about facial expressions and tell them apart, which should help them with everyday interactions.

Addie, a volunteer from the audience, challenges the robot to recognize a series of different facial expressions, and we see how Zeno has a camera that tracks forty specific points on Addie's face and uses machine learning to work out from these what the facial expression is.

'So, you can get through all sorts of intentions and emotions without uttering a word,' says Scott. But all of these interactions rely on our senses to pick up the messages. As Scott nears the end of her second Lecture, she poses a tantalizing question. What if we could communicate silently, directly from brain to brain instead?

Addie puts Zeno through its paces

It turns out that if an alien species has figured out how to do this, they could already be decoding human thought. Along with the sound of laughter, the *Voyager* space probes, which were launched forty years before Scott's Lecture, also contained another, fuzzy-sounding recording. 'There's a sound on the records not many people know about,' says Scott. These are the recordings of the electrical signals from someone's brain converted into sound waves. An alien species might be able to decode some of them, Scott suggests.

Closer to home, some scientists are already starting to do just that. Onto the stage comes Dr Ioannis Zoulias from the University of Reading, and we are also introduced to a young volunteer called Hannah, who is being filmed at the other end of the Royal Institution wearing an EEG headset that is reading her brainwaves. The challenge will be to see whether Hannah can send a message directly from her brain to her mother, Rashima, who has also joined Scott on stage.

The message Hannah is trying to send is a simple one; there are two coloured squares on a screen in front of her. When she looks at one of them, a blindfolded Rashima, who has each hand hovering over a different coloured buzzer, is going to receive the message via electrodes on her arms telling her which one to press. 'The computer will interpret her brainwaves and stimulate either Rashima's right or left arm,' Scott says. On a big screen in the Lecture Theatre, the audience is silently fixated on Hannah as she looks at the red square, and the signal is passed from Hannah's brain to her mother's arm. Eventually, Rashima presses the red button in front of her to the sound of rapturous applause. Impressive as the demonstration is, it's early days for brain decoding. 'We are nowhere near being able to communicate complex thoughts via an electrical signal. But every science has to start somewhere,' Scott says.

In her final Lecture, Scott pushes the limits of communication even further, asking whether we are alone in our ability to share our thoughts with others through language, or whether we will one day be able to talk to other species.

To begin to answer the question, Scott compares the human brain to that of a canary. Canaries and other songbirds also communicate using complex sounds, with rhythm, pitch and rate, much like human speech. The most impressive can learn over a thousand different songs. But unlike us, songbirds can't chop up their songs and rearrange them to create new meaning, so it's unlikely their vocalizations contain anything as complex as the meaning in human speech.

Some birds do better, however. Scott's next guest is a green Amazon parrot called Helli. She knows about ten human words, as well as other sounds, and she gains the respect of the audience when she does an impression of a bomb falling, then exploding. This ability lies with the fact that there are special brain regions dedicated to the way we learn and produce the sounds we make with our voices, and it turns out birds and humans share many of these.

Scott invites her colleague Dr Ricci Hannah to shed more light on these brain areas, accompanied by comedian Robin Ince. What is about to happen is a 'temporary state of affairs' Scott reassures Ince, as Dr Hannah sets up his equipment for a dramatic demonstration. 'I thought you were going to prove that I'm less intelligent than a parrot,' Ince jokes.

Scott explains that a magnetic field is going to be used to pass a current through Ince's brain, changing his brain activity without needing to do anything

Robin Ince prepares to have his brain zapped

invasive. It's a technique called transcranial magnetic stimulation, and being able to temporarily switch off specific brain areas in this way can be very useful.

'We can use it to probe how different parts of the brain play a role in different aspects of behaviour – in this case, speech,' Hannah says.

Holding the magnet near to Ince's head, Hannah asks the comedian to recite the months of the year, but he only makes it to April when Hannah switches on the current and his words instantly turn into babbling gibberish. The audience finds it hilarious, but Ince is spooked. 'That is weird,' he finally manages to say.

The area of the brain that Hannah has been targeting is the inferior frontal gyrus on the left side of the brain, which is important for planning or controlling speech. When he zaps another part of the brain, Ince is able to speak just fine, showing just how precisely we now understand where speech comes from in the brain.

Given this growing understanding, Scott ponders the question of whether we will ever be able to communicate with other species, or even with robots. Some computers seem quite good at understanding what we say, and many of us now command our phones using our voice or have voice-activated personal assistant devices around the home. It's incredibly hard to overestimate how quickly the field of speech processing – on which Scott did her PhD – is developing, she says.

Even so, there are huge challenges in getting computers to truly understand our speech. The first is a familiar issue to anyone who has tried to learn a new language – at the beginning it sounds like a constant stream of noises and it's impossible to tell where one word ends and another begins. How can robots convert the stream of sounds we make into meaningful words? This problem of speech recognition is known within science as a 'ridiculously difficult question', Scott jokes.

Even if computers, like our phones and personal assistants, do learn to understand individual words, a crucial ingredient of how we communicate is not just what we say but how we say it. Showing the audience a model of the brain, Scott explains that the left-hand side is interested in decoding speech and how we control our voices. The right side is much more interested in the other things that are going on, such as 'Who we are talking to? Are they being emotional? Are they telling a brilliant joke?'

To truly have a meaningful conversation with a machine, we would therefore need to build in this right-hand brain. In particular, the intonation in

EYEWITNESS

Fran Scott (no relative of the Lecturer) is a science content producer at the Royal Institution, and a science television presenter. Sophie Scott's Lectures were the first she worked on. 'I'm used to shooting in a massive studio, with all of the studio facilities around me. But I knew that obviously here we film in a 200-year-old theatre with a door that's a normal-size door. In 2017, for Sophie Scott there was a Barton's pendulum (which is used to demonstrate the phenomenon of resonance). Now, that prop was bigger in every dimension than the door we had to get it through. So it was wider, taller, and I was thinking 'How are we going to do this?' We had it half collapsed and had to angle it through the door, and also we had a back panel. So we had to snake around this back panel, in through the door, and then erect it in the theatre. And I remember the producer saying, 'Can you do this faster?' and we were like, 'No, not really!'

speech, which is dealt with by this right hemisphere, adds emotion and enhances specific meanings, and it is processed very differently in the brain than the words themselves. 'Often it can be as important, if not more important, to the real meaning of what somebody is saying,' Scott says.

Some computers are starting to rise to the challenge. 'For our last demonstration I'm going to look at something really amazing – a computer that can read emotions from human voices,' says Scott as she heads into the hallway to meet a computer called Olly.

'Hey, Olly, what's the weather like in London today?' our Lecturer asks in a sad voice and an icon of a crying face instantly pops onto the computer screen, showing that it understands not just the words, but the emotion behind them. 'He could be a digital assistant that is really understanding how you feel, not just what you're saying,' Scott says.

As another series comes to an end, Scott returns to the *Voyager* probes, taking her young audience back to the moment she decided to become a scientist forty years earlier. Watching Carl Sagan describe his work on the space probes in the 1977 Christmas Lectures 'literally set me on course to standing here today,' she says. Those probes are now billions of miles away from Earth, carrying the golden records that contain greetings in fifty-five human languages.

The big question Scott leaves us with is whether there is another life form out there that could crack our code. 'If they have brains like ours, maybe one day we could have conversations with them,' she says. But for that to happen, one thing is sure, she tells the audience. 'I hope you've realized it will need to have an incredible brain, at least as incredible as your brains, to do so.'

EPILOGUE

Our understanding of the brain is a paradoxical one. It is easy to take for granted today the many technologies we have at our disposal that allow us to peer inside our heads and witness the brain in action. Thanks to these and many other advances, we have a clearer picture than ever before about how this infinitely complex organ works. And yet so many mysteries remain, not least what happens when things go wrong – with the causes of many mental health problems, and diseases of the brain such as Parkinson's and Alzheimer's, still beyond our reach.

If this can seem frustrating we can take some comfort from how much we have learned and how far we have come since the first Lecture in this book in 1926 to the most recent in 2017. In the early days, scientists were still uncovering the rudimentary mechanics of the nervous system, such as how an electrical signal travels from the brain to control the muscles.

As our understanding grew, some common topics emerged. The senses feature heavily because they are our window onto the world; in particular, vision. How does the brain take what we see, just physical light, and turn it into something rich and meaningful? This line of enquiry revealed early on that things aren't always as they seem, a theme that features in many of the Lectures, and one that leads to some bigger fundamental questions we still seek to answer today about who is really in control, and the very nature of reality. Another recurring idea is that the brain is more than the sum of its parts, somehow taking a bunch of electrical and chemical processes and conjuring up our very sense of self. There's no guarantee we will ever find the answer – it might simply be beyond the capabilities of the human mind to completely understand itself.

But what is also abundantly clear through this series of fascinating talks is that the journey is far from over. The time for neuroscience is now, and understanding the brain is arguably the most exciting scientific endeavour of this generation. There are still rich pickings to be had, and no doubt by the time the next Christmas Lecture series about the brain rolls around, another cohort of young people will be astounded once again by the great leaps in our understanding. With some luck we will also be closer to solving some of the most pressing mental health issues facing society. And who knows, perhaps the very brain to solve them will be sitting right there in the audience.

AUTHOR'S NOTE

I didn't grow up watching the Christmas Lectures, but first encountered them through a work-experience placement as a student (culminating in a starring role as a carrot) and later went on to work on them as part of the production team. From the first day it was obvious how cherished the Lectures are and how many people they enthuse about science each year; I'm so grateful to now be part of that club.

I'd like to thank everyone at the RI who has been involved with this book, especially Charlotte New, Liina Hultgren and Dom McDonald. An enormous thank you to Jo Stansall at Michael O'Mara for her patience and understanding as I foolishly tried to deliver a book and a baby at the same time. Special thanks to Bruce Hood, Colin Blakemore, Kevin Warwick and Fran Scott for sharing their experiences of the Lectures with me. And thank you to Alok for always supporting and believing in me, to Amelie for keeping me company throughout this whole process, and to Remy for his unending curiosity; a daily reminder of the wonders of the developing brain.

Chapter 1

A. V. Hill's Lectures formed the basis for his book, *Living Machinery*, which was published in 1927 by G. Bell & Sons Ltd. Direct quotes are taken from that, as well as newspaper accounts of the Lectures and from the official programme that accompanied the series.

Chapter 2

In 1949, Hamilton Hartridge's book, *Colours and How We See Them*, was published by G. Bell & Sons Ltd, and based on his Lectures. Direct quotes come from this and the RI programme.

Chapter 3

Direct quotes for this chapter come from Frederic Bartlett's book, *The Mind at Work and Play*, published by George Allen and Unwin Ltd in 1951, which was based on these Lectures, as well as the RI pamphlet about the Lectures and various newspaper reports.

Chapter 4

Gregory's Lectures were televised but there are no known recordings or records of the contents of the Lectures. Instead, this chapter was pieced together from the Lecture programme that accompanied this series, as well as two of Gregory's books, which contain material from the Lectures: *The Intelligent Eye*, published in 1970, and *Eye and Brain*, published in 1966 (both by Weidenfeld & Nicolson). Direct quotes were taken from these (for *Eye and Brain*, excerpts © 2015, CCC Republication). Further biographical information comes from various papers published in *Nature* and *Biographical Memoirs of Fellows of the Royal Society*.

Chapters 5–10

Direct quotes from Heinz Wolff, Colin Blakemore, Susan Greenfield, Kevin Warwick, Bruce Hood and Sophie Scott were taken from video recordings of the Lectures.

PICTURE CREDITS

Page 1: photo from the 2018 Lectures given by Professor Alice Roberts and Professor Aoife McLysaght; Paul Wilkinson Photography

Page 8: lecture programme (front cover); from the collection of the Royal Institution (RI MS AD 06/A/03/A/1926)

Page 10: photograph of Hill with his children, David and Polly; originally reproduced in the *Illustrated London News*, 8 January 1927 © Illustrated London News Ltd / Mary Evans

Page 14: galvanometer picture from plate section in *Living Machinery* by A.V. Hill; G. Bell & Sons Ltd., London 1946

Page 15: galvanometer diagram from *Living Machinery* (see above)

Page 25: diagram of glass prism experiment, from *Colours and How We See Them*, H. Hartridge; G. Bell & Sons Ltd, London 1949

Page 26: Lecture picture of infrared experiment from *Colours and How We See Them* (see above)

Page 28: page from the *Illustrated London News*, featuring Hamilton's Lectures; originally reproduced in the *Illustrated London News*, 4 January 1947 © Illustrated London News Ltd / Mary Evans

Page 30: lecture programme (front cover); from the collection of the Royal Institution (RI MS AD 06/A/03/A/1946)

Page 42: lecture programme (front cover); from the collection of the Royal Institution (RI MS AD 06/A/03/A/1948)

Page 44: photograph of Bartlett and Lecture audience; Keystone / Hutton Archive / Getty Images

Page 47: reading experiment from *The Mind at Work and Play*, Sir Frederic Bartlett; George Allen & Unwin Ltd, London 1951

Page 50: ambiguous figure, 'My Wife and My Mother-in-Law' by cartoonist W. E. Hill; Wikimedia Commons / 'Puck' 6 November 1915

Page 58: horse and rider image experiment from *The Mind at Work and Play* (see above)

Page 62: photograph of Gregory and eye model; photographer WDG Cox

Page 69: photograph of Gregory demonstrating impossible triangle; photographer WDG Cox

Page 71: photograph of Gregory with audience; photographer WDG Cox

Page 71: Kanizsa triangle; Fibonacci / CC 3.0 / Wikimedia Commons

Page 73: photograph of Gregory during one of his Lectures; photographer WDG Cox

Page 75: lecture programme (front cover); from the

collection of the Royal Institution (RI MS AD 06/A/03/A/1967)

Page 76: letter from Gregory to RI director George Porter; from the collection of the Royal Institution (NCUAS/C/1068) / Richard Gregory Estate

Page 81: lecture programme (front cover); from the collection of the Royal Institution (RI MS AD 06/A/03/A/1975)

Page 86: still from Lecture 3; BBC Motion Gallery / Getty Images

Page 91: still from Lecture 6; BBC Motion Gallery / Getty Images

Page 93: still from Lecture 6; BBC Motion Gallery / Getty Images

Page 95: Wolff's list of possible Lecture titles; from the collection of the Royal Institution (NCUAS/C/1092) / Heinz Wolff Estate

Page 96: letter from Wolff to the TV producer of the series; from the collection of the Royal Institution (NCUAS/C/1092) / Heinz Wolff Estate

Page 98: lecture programme (front cover); from the collection of the Royal Institution (RI MS AD 06/A/03/A/1982)

Page 106: still from Lecture 4; BBC Motion Gallery / Getty Images

Page 108: still from Lecture 6; BBC Motion Gallery / Getty Images

Page 112: still from Lecture 6; BBC Motion Gallery / Getty Images

Page 115: letter from Blakemore to the TV producer for the series; from the collection of the Royal Institution (NCUAS/C/1140) / Sir Colin Blakemore

Page 117: lecture programme (front cover); from the collection of the Royal Institution (RI MS AD 06/A/03/A/1994)

Page 120: photograph of Greenfield and python; from the collection of the Royal Institution, photographer unknown

Page 121: photograph of Greenfield and owl; from the collection of the Royal Institution, photographer unknown

Page 125: still from Lecture 4; BBC Motion Gallery / Getty Images

Page 134: letter from Peter Day to St James' Palace; from the collection of the Royal Institution (RI MS AD 06/A/03/C/1994)

Page 135: letter from Greenfield to Peter Day; from the collection of the Royal Institution (RI MS AD 06/A/03/C/1994) / Baroness Susan Greenfield

Page 138: still from Lecture 2; Channel 4

Page 140: still from Lecture 2; Channel 4

Page 142: photograph of Kismet the robot © Jared C. Benedict on 16 October 2015 / CC-BY-SA-2.5 / Wikimedia Commons

Page 146: still from Lecture 4; Channel 4

Page 148: flashcards from Lecture; from the collection of the Royal Institution (RI MS AD 06/A/03/C/2000)

Page 156: letter from Greenfield to Warwick; from the collection of the Royal Institution (RI MS AD 06/A/03/C/2000

Page 158: ticket from Lecture; from the collection of the Royal Institution (RI MS AD 06/A/03/C/2011)

Page 162: photograph from the Lectures; Paul Wilkinson Photography

Page 163: sketch of Ames room; from the collection of the Royal Institution (RI MS AD 06/A/03/C/2011)

Page 164: photograph from the Lectures; Paul Wilkinson Photography

Page 168: photograph from the Lectures; Paul Wilkinson Photography

Page 178: ticket from the Lectures; from the collection of the Royal Institution (RI MS AD 06/03/C/2017)

Page 181: photograph from the Lectures; Paul Wilkinson Photography

Page 186: photograph from the Lectures; Paul Wilkinson Photography

Page 190: photograph from the Lectures; Paul Wilkinson Photography

INDEX

(Page numbers in *italic* refer to photographs and illustrations)

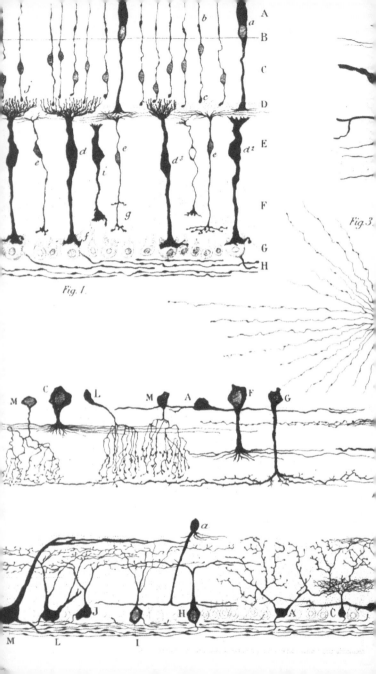

Fig. 1.

Fig. 3.